18,95

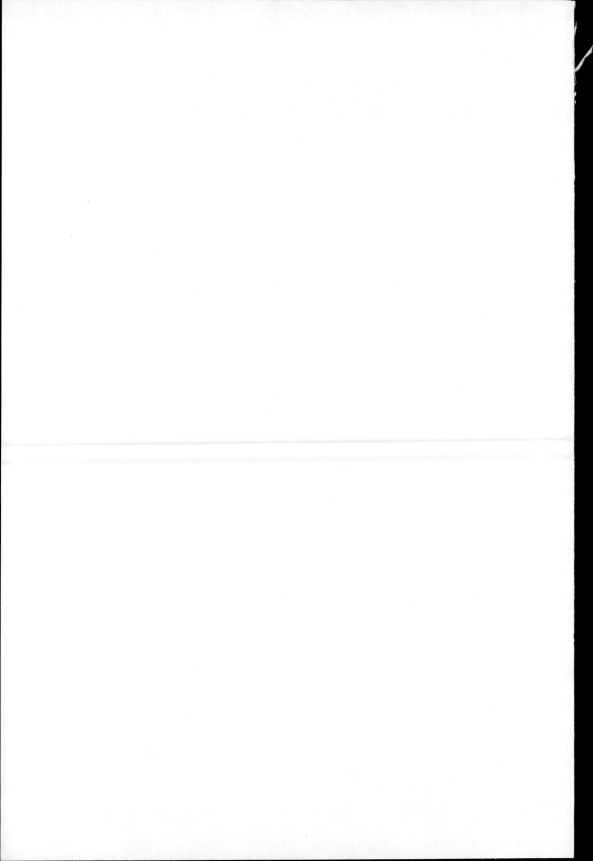

Controlling
the New Inflation

Controlling the New Inflation

Thomas J. Dougherty

LexingtonBooks
D.C. Heath and Company
Lexington, Massachusetts
Toronto

Dedicated to Allard K. Lowenstein
1929–1980

Library of Congress Cataloging in Publication Data

Dougherty, Thomas J.
  Controlling the new inflation.

  Includes index.
    1. Wage-price policy—United States.   2. Price regulation—United States.
  3. Inflation (Finance)—United States.   I. Title.
  HC110.W24D68   332.4'15'0973   80–8962
  ISBN 0-669-04512-8   AACR2

Copyright © 1981 by D.C. Heath and Company

Published simultaneously in Canada

Printed in the United States

International Standard Book Number: 0-669-04512-8

Library of Congress Catalog Card Number: 80-8962

Contents

Contents

List of Figures
and Tables

Preface: The New Deal, the New Spirit, and the New Inflation

During Franklin Delano Roosevelt's first administration, this nation was confronted with a completely novel situation for which the traditional, commonly accepted philosophies afforded no guide. FDR understood that the situation and the electorate would respond to a leader with a self-confident, experimental temper. Although his early New Deal trials and errors, principally the National Recovery Act, may have had only slight effects on recovery, they signaled a method that, in the end, achieved a certain measure of recovery, revived the American spirit, and bequeathed to later generations several measures of permanent value.

Today, the severity of the new inflation and its persistence, despite growing unemployment, has completely shaken people's faith in economic orthodoxies. During 1980, for example, inflation was lowered to 12 percent from peak levels of 20 percent only at the cost of America's seventh recession since World War II, while no long-run reforms were put in place to avoid resurgence of higher inflation—to be followed by an inevitable eighth recession to slightly dampen it.

Again, as in FDR's time, a completely novel situation calls for an era of bold initiative and considerable experimentation if there is to be any hope of simultaneously lowering the rates of inflation and unemployment. However, national economic policy—to say nothing of foreign policy—is adrift and has been adrift through a series of administrations.

In times like these, a transition of government should be a shock of ideas, a conversion experience. Yet, presidential administrations come and go with little understanding of and little beneficial effect upon the new inflation.

There are many reasons for this, but surely chief among them is the lack of a broad consensus about what government should do and who in government should do it. In the absence of such a broad consensus, the Congress and the president are institutionally incapable of effective action.

It is hard to identify many instances in this century when a president was able to implement sweeping social or economic reforms. In each of those that traditionally come to mind—the New Freedom of Woodrow Wilson's first years, FDR's first-term New Deal, and Lyndon Johnson's Great Society programs—the president came to office with a sweeping electoral mandate following a period in which a broad consensus had developed around the man and, to varying degrees, around the manner of tackling the major issues of the day.

The switch in control of the U.S. Senate following the Republican land-slide in the 1980 election of Ronald Reagan reflected a rejection of ossified New Deal liberalism and a consensus that government was so ineffectual that it was best reduced to a more limited role. It did not, however, reflect a consensus about what government can and should do about the debilitating cycles of ever-higher inflation and stagnation. Rather, it signaled that, if government cannot make up its mind about what to do, and do it force-fully, it is better that government do less. In other words, I believe, Americans called "time out" while they regrouped.

Lacking a programmatic consensus, our recent elections have perpetuated the policy stalemate. This book, therefore, is written as an exer-cise in applied political economy, with a view to the late 1980s and the 1990s, when younger Americans will have replaced our present leadership. As such, it is a brazen attempt at persuasion addressed to my own genera-tion, a generation that gained political consciousness between John F. Ken-nedy's inaugural address and the murders at Kent State. This book attempts to raise questions about some matters (such as whether wage and price con-trols work) that our present leaders consider well settled ("they don't work") and to suggest in considerable illustrative detail other elements of alternative economic policy. It aims at consensus-building.

Simple metaphors, the vehicles by which human thought advances, have a special magic in the politics of consensus formation. It is a telling commentary on our times to compare, for example, the metaphors chosen by FDR, Jimmy Carter, and Ronald Reagan to symbolize their respective transitions of government.

The New Deal was a powerful mixed metaphor of progressive conser-vatism: a new deal from a government-backed deck of cards—an image borrowed from the quintessential American game of poker; conservative because only the deal (opportunity) was new, not the distribution of chips (wealth). Life, like the game of poker, would still be risky, but those who had fallen on hard luck would be given another chance; and the government oversight of the deal (for example, through the SEC and Federal Reserve) and government insurance of the house (for instance, through the FDIC) assured a greater measure of fair play.

In contrast, Jimmy Carter's metaphor lacked programmatic content. Jimmy Carter's New Spirit (a now-forgotten image) importantly empha-sized a civil-religious mood change following the corruption of Watergate. Engineer-politician Jimmy Carter came to power as a result of his mastery of the mechanics of national mood. But he was particularly ill-equipped to fashion economic policy in difficult times. He introduced more concept-ually inconsistent economic strategies per year in office than any other modern president—itself a sign of uncertain times—with no good effect. However, to the limited extent he followed a consistent theme, it was decidedly not a liberal one. On economic matters, Carter's policies were indistinguishable from Gerald Ford's shoulder-shrugging acceptance of recession and unemployment as painful methods of slightly dampening inflation. As discussed in this book, planned recession is not only a painful method but ultimately a self-defeating one. Each recession has been followed by resurgent new inflation, with the result that, in the next cycle, both recession and inflation have been more severe than in the previous cycle.

The Reagan landslide registered voter disgust with the evaporation of the New Deal into the New Spirit that Carter had engineered. All Reagan offered was a new attitude (or, ironically, a "spirit") of limited government. He would do even less than the incompetent Carter, but would at least, be acting intentionally. He would not repeal the New Deal, but he would gut the Great Society.

Reagan's inaugural image, a New Beginning, is an amnesic metaphor of Disney-like oversimplification. Does anyone believe, to quote James Wieghart[1] of the *New York Daily News,* that the energy crisis, pollution, structural unemployment, and pervasive inflation "lend themselves to solution by a weak central government which is subservient to an unfettered private sector"? Luckily, those who do, or out of self-interest pretend to, will have their chance between 1981 and 1985 to show that less government means less inflation and less unemployment. A Republican president, a Republican Senate and a House dominated by the old coalition of Republicans and conservative Democrats will have an unfettered chance to prove it. I believe they will fail. The economy is not a Disney world.

Indeed, the popular resentment that expressed itself in the Reagan landslide is a recognition that, on one critical problem after another, a whole generation of leaders has now failed America. That resentment haunts the Republican successors. The times need a Graham Greene of presidents, prepared when necessary to make a "journey without maps." Naval Academy graduate Jimmy Carter was, from the start, constitutionally and habitually incapable of that. This is not to say that his confidence in his own integrity was not well founded, but simply, to state the obvious, that such self-confidence was no substitute for programmatic courage. Now, the stalemate continues. Reagan's courage is antiprogammatic.

Yet the American mood is increasingly beyond political manipulation. For the majority of Americans today, inflation is the bellwether of government performance. When milk costs more than two dollars a gallon, no amount of sophistry from Republican or Democrat can assuage the thought that all children are being cheated out of material well-being while increasingly many are already badly undernourished. The "night that came to the Cumberlands" is spreading across the land. All our neighborhoods are taking on the look of the "Other America." The future looks small indeed.

A Congressional Budget Office study predicts that the price of oil will be $84 per barrel by 1990. If past experience is any guide, the CBO will significantly underestimate, principally because no one can forecast the timing or effects of discontinuous jolts to political equilibrium in the Middle East.

In one very limited sense, though, the American economy has shown remarkable ability to cope with such jolts. Its method of coping is called the new inflation. So resilient is the American economy that five years after the oil embargo and price hikes of the Yom Kippur War, the real price of gasoline in the United States (that is, adjusted for inflation) was *less* than immediately after the price hikes. Generally speaking, the price of everything else in the United States went up faster than oil after the Yom Kippur War, so that, by 1979, oil was cheaper in real terms than it was in 1974. But this superficial resilience does not hide the enormous erosion of productivity, savings, and the American standard of living that took place during the intervening recession and inflation. Nor did such classic economic disequilibrium adjustment restore the pre-Yom Kippur War real price of oil. Rather, in 1979–1980, OPEC, recognizing that the new inflation had undercut the value of the initial price hikes, announced an equally dramatic second jolt to oil prices, propelling heating oil to well over one dollar per gallon and precipitating yet another recession and another era of secondary price adjustment, with all the attendant injury to productivity and welfare. There is no end in sight to this process of oil jolt, recession, secondary price adjustment, oil jolt. Indeed, one is only left to guess at this point how long the process will take (recession and inflation, adjusting to the 1979–1980 oil-price jolt) before the next jolt to $60 per barrel of oil. My guess is that oil will be $60 by 1984.

The question arises—especially if (light years ago, it seems) you marched on Washington, if you fought in Vietnam believing you were fighting for something at the clear-minded direction of informed leadership, if you are now underemployed or your reform-mindedness is undertapped—will the coming generation be willing to follow floundering national leadership as it complacently uses (antiblack, antiwoman) recessionary policy to pass on the effects of continuing oil-price hikes to $84 a barrel and beyond? No, we are not.

When Jimmy Carter's economic policies are seen for what they were, it is patent that liberalism has not failed. Liberalism has not been tried.

This book does not pretend to have all the answers, but it does dare to be intellectually aggressive and fairly specific. It assumes that the Roosevelt-Truman-Kennedy-Johnson idea of affirmative government in pursuit of intelligent public purpose offers greater hope to the country than laissez-faire recidivism. But that idea must be taken out of mothballs after fifteen years and adapted to novel problems. This book's thesis is that controlling the new inflation turns upon our ability to stabilize prices in food, energy, housing, and health. To that end, an analysis of wage and price controls and specific longer-run sectoral strategies is set forth, aimed at stabilizing prices in these basic necessities. Although these ideas are presented in some detail, in order to raise and treat many issues that are often neglected so that special interests will not be offended, the detail sketched here is not that of a map for the journey of our generation; the journey remains one without maps. Rather, these details are principles of applied topography that, it is believed, could be of some service if the terrain continues to be as rough as it has been in the last decade and to be shaped by the same powerful forces.

In summary, the motivating ideas for this book can be simply stated: (1) Just as a novel situation confronted architects of the New Deal, a new inflation confronts us today. (2) Although Carter's New Spirit signaled a civil-religious mood change following the corruption of Watergate, the New Deal evaporated into the New Spirit—an administration devoid of programmatic content. The Republican New Beginning was actually a continuation of twelve years of conservative economic policy by Nixon, Ford, and Carter. (3) What programs are appropriate? The causes of the new inflation are not generalized, and neither are its long-run cures. Mere budget cutting will not significantly reduce an inflation that is not primarily caused by deficits. (4) One generalized anti-inflation program—wage and price control—has been unduly criticized, however, since it can provide short-run relief at much lower social cost than recession, the alternative generalized cure. (5) For the longer run, however, each primary cause of inflation (food, energy, housing, and health costs—the leading inflationary sectors) requires a particularized, not a generalized, response. (6) Thus, rather than mere tight money and tax cuts, we need to consider, respectively, grain-export management, short-term gasoline rationing (either by coupon or tax) immediately following each OPEC jolt together with a mix of new energy-source programs, credit allocation toward the housing sector, innovative mortgage lending (such as equity sharing), and reordered budgetary incentives in health care (through hospital-cost containment, for example).

Note

1. As quoted by Arthur Schlesinger, Jr., in the *Wall Street Journal,* Thursday, November 20, 1980, at p.26.

You talk about turning down thermostats. We have turned down thermostats in New Hampshire and New England long ago. They are down to 65 and in many cases they are lower than that. People are watching their paychecks disappear into their oil burner, week after week, after week.... I have just come from New Hampshire and it was about 3 degrees up there last night, and it's been a cold winter. We can't burn recommendations, we can't burn reports, we can't convert them into wood pellets or solid waste pellets or convert them into energy.... The national energy plan that came up here was totally deficient, was totally deficient on transportation. Gasoline mileage standards proposed would save less gas than would be saved if it rains on the Fourth of July. We wanted to switch so New England could burn coal when the coal conversion program was to switch to coal.... The administration has opposed money to revitalize the rail beds, so there is only one way to get coal into New England now and that is to fly it in.

—Senator John A. Durkin, interrupting remarks of David J. Bardin, Economic Regulatory Administration, Department of Energy, February 5, 1979, before the Subcommittee on Energy Regulation, U.S. Senate Committee on Energy and National Resources.

There is nothing more difficult to carry out, nor more doubtful of success, nor more dangerous to handle, than to initiate a new order of things.
—Machiavelli

Acknowledgments

The National Center for Economic Alternatives, its codirectors, Gar Alperovitz and Jeff Faux, Professor Glen Nelson of the University of Minnesota, U.S. Court of Appeals Judge Stephen Breyer, and members of the staff of the *Harvard Journal on Legislation* all assisted, at one time or another, in my research for this book. The views expressed are solely my own.

Part I:
Controls—And the
Basic Necessities

The Consumer Price Index and the prime rate have topped annualized rates of over 20 percent in recent experience. Only 20 years ago, we considered 2 percent inflationary.

Economic policy is adrift. There is no coherent consensus in the administration, in the Congress, or among the public with respect to an appropriate policy response.

The economy is stagnating. In the early 1980s, for example, recession failed to check inflationary momentum, and recovery faltered. During the "recovery period" following the 1979–1980 recession, America's real economic growth rate never reached a sustained rate of 1.5 percent. That is extraordinarily low for a period of economic recovery. For example, in 1961, 1971, and 1975, years of economic recovery, real growth was 6 to 7 percent in the United States. Subnormal economic growth for an extended period of time erodes expectations and ultimately creates enormous social frictions. Wage demands have moved into routine ranges of 10 to 11 percent annually. Yet productivity has declined at an average annual rate of .4 percent since 1977. At near-stagnant growth rates, there is just not enough new national income created to go around. Meanwhile, the urban black male unemployment rate has stuck near 14 percent, twice that for whites.

We have seen how difficult it is to cut the budget, and in any event, as this book seeks to show, our inflationary problems are primarily due to other influences. That is not to say that budget cuts are not helpful. Any significant reduction in the $80 billion annual federal financing requirements (government borrowing to finance the nearly $1 trillion national debt) frees up credit for private investment uses. But the Congressional Budget Office has estimated that it would take a permanent $20 billion budget cut to reduce the inflation rate by one-half of one percent. It is difficult to effect such cuts without devastating many social programs, given the priority of defense.[1]

For example, in fiscal 1980 and 1981, federal expenditures *increased* by 17 percent and 14 percent, respectively. Of the approximately $700 billion in annual federal expenditures, approximately 67 percent are uncontrollable by the president; they are mandated by Congress. If one recognizes the special priority of defense expenditures (and assumes they cannot be cut), approximately 90 percent of federal expenditures are then uncontrollable. The remaining 10 percent are not fully controllable, but even if they were, it would have taken their complete elimination to balance the fiscal 1981 budget. To truly check nondefense expenditures, Congress would have to deeply cut entitlement programs such as Social Security and food stamps.

Still, budgetary responsibility, including sensitivity for transfer recipients' welfare, is important, even if not sufficient by itself, as a signal to the economy that sacrifice must be made. So, too, is a more consistent monetary policy. For example, from April to July 1980, within two-and-a-half months, the most sensitive of interest rates, the federal funds rate, dropped from 19 percent to 8 percent. In previous economic cycles, it usually took more than two years for interest rates to fall by 50 percent or more. Then, in late 1980, the rate jumped upward again. Such rapid swings in interest rates alternately ignite and halt credit creation, with shattering effects on business expectations.

Third, tax cut measures (not an inflationary Kemp-Roth bill, but lower rates—whether for the individual, the business, the saver, or the financial institution) are needed to offset the inflation tax of bracket-creep and taxes on inflation-created capital gains.

As important as budget reform, consistent monetary policy, and tax cuts (or full tax reform) are, they are beyond the scope of this book. They are already the subject of much debate. The purpose of this book is to rekindle interest in a now unfashionable anti-inflation tool—wage and price controls—and to try to shift the debate toward policies directly affecting the sectors where inflation has been, and continues to be, most severe—the necessities.

At times there have been dramatic shifts in the debate over wage and price controls.[2] In 1980, Barry Bosworth, former director of the Council on Wage and Price Stability, abandoned the "muddle-through" Carter administration tactics he helped design and called for wage-price-profit controls.[3] His reversal was followed by Brookings Institution president (and former Minneapolis Federal Reserve Bank chief) Bruce K. MacLaury. Otto E. Eckstein testified at about the same time that mandatory controls "deserve a serious look." House Banking Committee chairman Henry Reuss, Henry Kaufman, chief economist for Salomon Brothers, Felix Rohatyn, formerly head of the Municipal Assistance Corporation and influential investment banker at Lazard Freres, and *Business Week* magazine all joined in one way or another in calls for controls.

Liberal economists John Kenneth Galbraith, Robert Lekachman, and James Tobin, of course, have been urging controls for some years; and the liberal press, including the *Boston Globe,* joined by the *New Republic,* has advocated some form of freeze and phase authority. The AFL-CIO called for an equitable controls plan from October 1978 until mid–1980, when the recession deepened, slowing price increases somewhat, so that controls would have threatened the hope of wage catch-up.

A call for controls is a recognition that policies of budget-cutting, tight money, and ultimately planned recession hold virtually no hope for bringing near-hyperinflation under control.[4] Recessionary policy condemns the economy to future rounds of inflationary policy to end recession, followed by recessionary policy to dampen the resulting inflation. Moreover, as Bosworth pointed out, in each of these cycles the average levels of both unemployment and inflation are higher than in the previous cycle. That is, the "Phillips curve" (the trade-off curve between inflation and unemployment) shifts diagonally upward by the end of each cycle.

The 18 percent wholesale price increases of 1974 were lowered to 7 percent only by America's sixth and worst recession since World War II (9 million unemployed).[5] The overall rate of consumer price inflation declined to 5 percent in 1976 only because farm prices fell sharply and the pass-through of the 1973–1974 rise in energy prices was completed. Today, the unemployment level would have to rise to 10 percent (or more) according to Bosworth before there would be any significant effect on prices.[6] The 1979 energy-price increases will not fully pass through the economy until 1983, and in late 1980 farm prices were rising, not falling, in the wake of California floods, Florida frosts, midwest drought, and government "target" support price increases. In other words, in the early 1980s food price inflation was accelerating independent of oil-price jolt-inflation, which itself takes years to work its full effects on the economy.

The lack of consensus in professional opinion is not matched by public opinion. For example, the Gallup Poll, taken February 11, 1980, found a solid majority in favor of wage-price controls.

Two fundamental questions must be faced: (1) Are controls worth considering? (2) Can they be made to work? Answering the first question requires a recognition of the special nature of the current inflation. Answering the second requires a shift in the way we conceptualize our responses to it.[7]

Notes

1. Lester Thurow of MIT has pointed out that the overall governmental budget (federal, state, and local) is already in balance. In any event, a $50 billion budget cut in a $2.6 trillion economy, even with a powerful multiplier, would have only a moderate effect on inflation. If accompanied by reduced federal borrowing, it could lower short-term interest rates and thereby dampen interest-rate pressure on the general price level. But, as this analysis will show, the primary inflationary pressures would remain.

2. See, for example, Gar Alperovitz and Jeff Faux, codirectors of the National Center for Economic Alternatives, "Controls and the Basic Necessities," *Washington Post,* March 10, 1980.

3. Statement by Barry P. Bosworth before the Subcommitte on Eco-

nomic Stabilization of the Committee on Banking, Housing, and Urban Affairs, February 1, 1980.

4. Testifying on March 10, 1980, before the Senate Banking Committee, six former chairmen of the Council of Economic Advisors opposed mandatory controls *at that time* (Walter Heller, who advised John Kennedy; Arthur Okun and Gardner Ackley, who advised Lyndon Johnson; Paul McCracken and Herbert Stein, who advised Richard Nixon; and Alan Greenspan, who advised Gerald Ford). Heller and Okun did not rule out controls should tight budgets and tight money not work. See, also, Henry Kaufman, "Issues and Answers," Sunday, December 21, 1980; Professor Stephen A. Marglin, "After The Free Lunch: Wage-price controls," *Boston Globe,* Sunday, January 18, 1981; Felix Rohatyn, *New York Review of Books,* December 4, 1980.

5. Defina, "Labor and the Economy During 1975, Monthly Labor Review, January 1976 at 3, "Business Outlook", *Business Week,* January 26, 1976 at 19.

6. See George L. Perry, "Slowing the Wage-Price Spiral: The Macroeconomic View", *Brookings Papers on Economic Activity,* Vol. 2, 1978 at 285.

7. See, also, Dougherty, "Sector by Sector Anti-Inflation Legislation Proposed Amendments to the Council on Wage and Price Stability," 13 *Harvard Journal on Legislation* 363, February 1976.

1 Are Controls Worth Considering?

The new inflation is among the most serious threats to this nation's economic order and democratic system since World War II. It causes serious dislocations in the flow of economic activity. The uncertainty and the mistakes of investment planning that result significantly contribute to slowed productivity growth and capacity imbalances.[1] Inflation's distributive effects are neither systematic nor just. On the whole, it distributes income away from fixed-income groups, including those whose return on savings is fixed, and from workers and businesses whose economic power is weak, toward those with greater power and, given the progressive rate of the federal income tax, toward the federal government.[2]

Other unforeseeable effects also contribute to an inflationary psychology, which erodes the confidence of those who put their trust in the traditional order, hampers the effectiveness of fiscal, monetary, and other government policies, and poisons morale.

A review of past government attempts to slow inflation, and of the particular nature of the current inflation, suggests the need to seriously consider wage-price controls and other longer-run reforms. Past experience indicates the major problems and risks of controls. But the lessons learned in those periods can also be used to avoid or overcome some of the problems. No incomes policy can succeed in the face of shortages. The Nixon-period effort to use controls as a substitute for fiscal-monetary restraint was a mistake that led to distortion exacerbating the supply problem. But, as Bosworth stated, "There is still the possibility that a combination of controls and demand restraint can reduce the magnitudes of unemployment and idle capacity substantially below those required by a policy of relying on demand restraint [recession] alone".[3] The following discussion sets out the argument in detail.[4]

The Kennedy Wage-Price Guidelines

From 1960 to 1964, the Consumer Price Index was reasonably stable, averaging a 1.2 percent annual increase. Unemployment, however, averaged 5.8 percent from 1954 to 1963.[5] The Kennedy Administration felt that 6 percent unemployment was too high for an equilibrium value, so it set about to use fiscal and monetary policy to reduce that figure. However, uneasy about the

5

possibility of inflation, the administration instituted wage-price guide-lines.[6]

The guidelines were based on an estimation that the average annual rate of productivity increase during 1957–1962 had been 3.2 percent. If wages rose 3.2 percent annually, unit labor costs would remain stable and so would prices. In industries where productivity gains were less than 3.2 percent, prices could rise to pay a higher real-wage bill; in industries where productivity gains exceeded 3.2 percent, prices should fall. Regardless of theory, the guidelines were largely ignored in practice. By mid–1966, they had gradually collapsed as many union leaders began boasting to their members and to the public that the latest settlements were exceeding the guidelines.[7].

Among other problems, faulty projections about the relative labor-costs and price-levels doomed the program to failure. Implicit in the goal that unit labor costs and prices remain constant was the assumption that labor's share in national income would also remain constant (its slice of the national income pie would not increase or decrease relative to that of investors). However, profits rose at an annual rate of 11 percent during 1961–1965, whereas total wages rose only five percent.[8]

Profits rose faster than wages for two reasons. First, the national guidelines were set too low. Productivity in the manufacturing sector grew at approximately 4 percent per year, but almost no industries cut prices. Therefore, unit labor costs fell while prices stayed the same, and profit margins increased.[9] Second, in 1965 non-farm wholesale prices rose 1.3 percent, whereas they should have been falling with falling unit labor costs. Consequently, the spread between price and unit labor costs widened even further.[10]

In 1966, food prices rose about ten percent. Labor leaders called for 6 percent pay increases in upcoming negotiations, and many industries raised prices further in anticipation of large wage settlements. The guidelines had failed.[11]

The Nixon Economic Stabilization Program

In the late 1960s, inflation in the United States reached what was then considered a severe level. The Consumer Price Index accelerated from an increase of 2.8 percent in 1966–1967 to roughly 6.0 percent in 1970–1971.[12]

Upon his election in 1968, President Nixon declared he would not seek nor use authority to control inflation directly.[13] In August of 1970, however, such authority was provided when the Democratic Congress passed the Economic Stabilization Act in the face of strong administration opposition.[14] This legislation was grounded, at least in part, in the realities of partisan politics. "The President's opponents apparently sought to place him in the position that they could criticize him if he failed to use [wage and price controls], or if he used them to criticize him for not having his heart in the exercise or for their ineffectual administration."[15] Responding to a deteriorating economic situation, the president first applied controls on March 29, 1971,[16] to the construction industry where first-year collective bargaining settlements were averaging 19 percent.[17]

The imposition of a comprehensive wage-price freeze, which followed on August 15, 1971, was the first general application of direct inflation controls in the peacetime history of the United States.[18] That such action was taken by a Republican Administration, whose economic rhetoric up until that time had been primarily revanchist, suggests the political uncertainty and tension which surrounded Nixon's new economic policy. Phase I marked the beginning of a series of phases and freezes that became known as the Nixon Administration's Economic Stabilization Program.

The new economic policy primarily sought to strengthen the dollar against other currencies, especially the yen and the mark, and to encourage economic expansion through investment credits to business.[19] The dollar had been overvalued for some time both against gold and against other major currencies; and the economy's general sluggishness had been widely noted.[20] The stimulus to investors, to exporters, and to industries subject to foreign competition was aimed at raising output and lowering unemployment from its then current level of 6.1 percent.[21] Wage and price controls were merely an adjunct to the expansionist program. They were intended as moderating checks, "to reduce inflationary consequences of the unprecedented devaluation rather than as a significant end in themselves."[22] This contradictory combination of controls and stimulation can be compared to holding down the kettle lid while turning up the flame beneath.

The Phase I freeze took effect immediately upon its promulgation by President Nixon on August 15, 1971.[23] The freeze order provided for the stabilization of prices, rents, wages, and salaries, for a period of 90 days. It also established the Cost of Living Council,[24] which was charged with the primary responsibility for administering the stabilization program and for recommending to the president additional policies and mechanisms to permit an orderly transition from the 90-day general price, rent, wage, and salary freeze to a more flexible and selective system of economic restraints.[25]

There is little disagreement that the comprehensive freeze did restrain wage and price increases in the short-run. The major price indices showed a marked deceleration during the freeze period. The Consumer Price Index rose at an annual rate of 1.6 percent from August to November 1971, as compared with 4.0 percent in the six months preceding the freeze.[26] The decline in the rate of increase in the Wholesale Price Index was even more dramatic: the index declined at an annual rate of almost 0.4 percent during the freeze, as compared with an annual rate of increase of 4.9 percent prior to the freeze.[27] The largest price increases occurred in the prices of foods, nondurable goods, services, and rent. The freeze did not cover most food prices, and some of the increase in the price of services and rent had occurred before the freeze.[28] This short-run success was, "facilitated by the fact that the freeze was imposed on a cool economy marked by considerable slack in the labor force and industrial capacity.[29]

The freeze had little or no effect on food prices, and the stability of food prices during August to November 1971 should not be attributed to the freeze.[30] However, much of the popular perception of the short-term success of the freeze was probably attributable to the stability of food prices.[31] That people thought the freeze was a successful device for checking food price inflation proved to be unfortunate in retrospect. In the longer-run, the "toughness" of the freeze "clearly contributed to the magnitude of the post-freeze 'bubble' that distorted wage and price movements in the first few months of Phase II and made it extremely difficult to maintain the credibility of the stabilization program."[32] From November 1971 through February 1972, the Consumer Price Index rose at an annual rate of 4.8 percent, the Wholesale Price Index by 6.9 percent, and the index of hourly earnings for private non-farm production workers by 9.4 percent.[33]

Phase II was announced on October 15, 1971,[34] and implemented on November 13, 1971.[35] The freeze on wages and prices was discontinued, and a system of flexible wage, price, and rent-controls was authorized. Price- and rent-controls were administered by a Price Commission, composed of seven public members, and wage restraints were managed by a tripartite Pay Board, comprised of five representatives of business, five representatives of labor, and five public members.[36] These two groups were independent of the Cost of Living Council, but were required to act in concert with it.[37]

Overall goals of Phase II included a halving of the rate of price inflation from 5 to 5.5 percent down to 2 or 3 percent and a growth in productivity of 3 percent. Combining these objectives with a ceiling on wage increases of 5.5 percent and an additional 0.7 percent for pensions and health and welfare benefits, the administration sought to tie wage guideposts to aggregate productivity gains and prices to unit labor costs on an industry by industry basis so that an overall target of 2.5 percent inflation might be achieved.[38]

Price and wage increases above those norms could be approved by the Pay Board or the Price Commission. The general price standard specified that prices could be increased over August 1971 levels not more than would be proportional to increases in costs. If prices were increased, however, a firm's profit margin in relation to sales could not exceed the average of the best two of the three fiscal years preceding August 1971,[39] Both the Pay Board and the Price Commission operated regionally from the offices of the Internal Revenue Service. The Construction Industry Stabilization Committee in the meantime continued functioning as a semiautonomous body subject to the condition that its wage norms were to be consistent with those of the Pay Board. The Cost of Living Council continued as the coordinating and policymaking body.[40]

As in Phase I, raw agricultural products were not controlled at all. Thus, "Phase II price and wage controls had little or no direct effect on price increases originating at the farm level."[41] The Phase II control scheme for food manufacturers was identical to that employed for the rest of the economy.[42] That is, food manufacturers' price increases were allowed if related to cost increases, subject to the further constraint that firm-wide historical profit margins not be exceeded.[43] Firms with over $100 million in annual sales volume were required to notify the Price Commission 30 days in advance of proposed price increases.[44]

During the implementation of Phase II, the fluctuation of food raw-material prices interferred with the smooth administration of a prenotified price control scheme, in which price increases had to be justified by cost. Firms subject to large and unforseeable fluctuation in raw-material costs were unable to make the nearly instantaneous adjustments necessary to avoid cost absorption. Such firms were exempted from prenotification, under a "volatile price authority" rule.[45]

The upward pressure on raw agricultural prices was soon aggravated by events on the other side of the globe. The U.S.S.R.'s production of total grains in 1972–1973 was only 156 million tons, 13 million tons less than in 1971–1972, which was in turn 5 million tons less than 1970–1971 production.[46] Nearly all of the decline took place in wheat. Such variation was not uncommon; nor was it uncommon for the Soviet Union to make large purchases in world markets to offset substandard production.[47] Soviet net imports in similar poor harvest years were as follows: 1963–1964, 5.8 million metric tons imported; 1965–1966, 3.7 million metric tons imported; 1971–1972, 2.2 million metric tons imported.

On July 8, 1972, the White House triumphantly announced the Soviet-American grain deal.[48] The U.S.S.R. agreed to purchase $750 million of grain during a three-year period beginning August 1, 1972, at least $200 million of which would be purchased in the first year.[49] The Soviet Union was granted a credit up to $500 million in a manner similar to other purchasers of agricultural products.[50]

Beginning in early July and continuing through early August the Soviet Union purchased an unprecedented 20 million tons of wheat and feed grains fully offsetting their short-fall in production.[51] Three-fourths of the purchases were of wheat, and the bulk of these purchases were made from private American export companies. From 1971–1972 to 1972–1973, Soviet grain consumption actually rose 2.7 percent, rather than decreasing as expected following substandard production.[52]

The Department of Agriculture had been pursuing a policy of subsidizing wheat exports and continued it throughout the period of the Russian purchases. The export subsidy was designed to maintain the U.S. competitive position in world trade while domestic producers were receiving higher prices. Exporters received a payment for the difference between the domestic price and the lower fixed world price of $60 per ton. In the third quarter of 1972, a total of about $300 million of U.S. taxpayers' money was expended to subsidize Soviet and other foreign wheat consumers.[53] The farm price of wheat reached $2.38 per bushel by December, but since many wheat growers had sold in June and July for $1.38 per bushel or less, speculators and exporters reaped windfalls of $1 per bushel or more.[54]

The U.S. Department of Agriculture announced a very restrictive wheat program for 1973 on July 17, 1972, despite the announcement of the Soviet grain deal a few days earlier. The Department's goal included a reduction of government stockpiles of grain and an improvement of farm incomes. Payments to farmers to set aside acreage—not to produce—were the maximum allowed by law.[55] This combination of inept policy decisions by Secretary Earl Butz and his department contributed to a new upswing in prices in 1973–1974. Furthermore, it resulted in needless costs to American taxpayers, as already mentioned, and in a loss of foreign exchange earnings due to the artificially depressed world grain prices.

In contrast, the effectiveness of Phase II controls on prices of non-agricultural goods at the aggregate level has been summarized as follows:

> Comparisons of actual changes in prices at the aggregate level, and estimates of what would have occurred under historical conditions without price and wage controls, indicate first, a significant reduction in the rate of inflation for consumer prices (around 2.0 percentage points) and, second, a much smaller impact on wholesale prices (no more than 0.5 percentage points).These conclusions seem to follow from a variety of different approaches using aggregate, private non-farm data.[56]

Productivity (output per hour of all persons in the private business sector) increased from 107.8 to 111.4.

The gross national product increased from $1,107.5 billion to $1,171.1 billion.

Total personal consumption expenditures increased from $668.2 billion to $733.0 billion.

Corporate profits, after tax, increased from $82 billion to $96.2 billion.

Capital expenditures for new plant and equipment increased from $81.21 billion to $88.44 billion.

Unemployment decreased from 5.9 percent to 5.6 percent.

Total employment increased from 86.9 million to 90 million.

The Federal Reserve Index of Industrial Production increased from 106.3 to 115.7.

New private housing starts increased from 2,052,200 to 2,356,600 units. (In contrast, housing starts fell to 1,200,000 units in 1980.)

FHA new-home mortgage rates decreased from 7.78 percent to 7.53 percent.

Total business sales increased from $116 billion to $130 billion.

The rate of increase of hospital expenditures fell 25 percent, and for the first and only year since 1950 the hospital industry did not grow faster than the general economy.[57] Phase II was a success—except for agriculture.

Phase III was established on January 11, 1973.[58] It involved a shift from the Phase II system of specific rules requiring cost justification and prior approval to a system of loose, self-administered standards. Rent was decontrolled entirely. The functions of the Price Commission and the Pay Board were merged into a reorganized Cost of Living Council.[59] The new Council was headed by Harvard economics professor John T. Dunlop, who had previously been the chairman of the Construction Industry Stabilization Committee. The looseness of the standards in Phase III is exemplified by one regulation allowing price increases above those attributable to cost increases whenever "necessary for efficient allocation of resources or to maintain adequate level of supply."[60]

A number of reasons have been given for the drastic shift from Phase II to Phase III: (1) the administration had always been opposed to controls and eagerly sought an alternative; (2) price controls were not working well in several industries such as lumber and textiles;[61] (3) the economy was approaching capacity-utilization in many sectors, creating the need for more flexibility in general price regulations; (4) a general belief on the part of Secretary of the Treasury George P. Schultz that even the best controls became ineffective or unmanageable over time.[62]

While the remainder of the economy was placed under a voluntary controls program, food-manufacturing prices continued to remain under mandatory controls. The cost pass-through system that comprised Phase II was continued during Phase III with minor modifications.[63] But, as in Phases I and II, "Phase III food price policy did not attempt systematically to restrain large increases in raw product prices."[64] The shortages induced by the inept action of the Department of Agriculture in 1972 were, therefore, free to work their effects on prices in the food sector.[65]

The easing of restraint in Phase III was followed by a price explosion. Wholesale prices increased at a rate of 12.5 percent annually over the first year of Phase III.[66] A sector-by-sector breakdown of the price advance reveals that 90 percent of the increase in the Wholesale Price Index during January to June 1973 was concentrated in four sectors: food, petroleum products, textiles, and lumber.[67] Food prices, for example, increased at the following seasonally-adjusted annual rates:[68]

November 1972	8.4
December 1972	−1.2
January 1973	25.2
February 1973	22.8
March 1973	28.8
April 1973	16.8
June 1973	10.8

On March 29th, the Nixon Administration imposed a ceiling on the prices of red meat at processing, wholesale, and retail levels.[69] Again, the raw agricultural product, cattle feed, was exempt.[70] On May 2, the Phase II requirement that major businesses prenotify the Cost of Living Council of price increases was reinstituted.[71] On June 13, 1973, a second general freeze, of 60 days' duration, was imposed,[72] but again, raw agricultural products were not frozen.[73] Despite these measures, the administration's efforts were soon overwhelmed by another foreign development with extensive domestic inflationary impact.

Between October 1973 and January 1974, the export price of Saudi Arabian light crude oil increased three and one-half fold. By the end of 1974, it was four times the level it had been prior to the Arab-Israeli War of 1973.[74] This was the single most inflationary event since World War II.[75] The Brookings Institution study of the immediate effects of the Organization of Petroleum Exporting Countries (OPEC) price hikes and governmental response to them has been summarized as follows:

> In sum, the price-raising effect of the oil crisis, following hard on an already accelerating inflation, attracted far more attention from the makers of economic policy in the industrial nations than did its depressing effects on aggregate demand. Monetary policies, far from being relaxed to offset the demand-reducing effects of the oil "excise tax", were tightened in an effort to moderate its inflationary impact. The tightening was particularly evident in the United States and Japan, but it was also observable to a lesser extent in most Western European countries. The forces leading to recession were strengthened further. By the end of 1974 the sharp fall in aggregate demand was clearly acting to decelerate inflation in every country except the United Kingdom. But the cost, in most countries, was the worst recession in thirty years.[76]

By 1975, the OPEC price increases had reduced the United States' real GNP by about $35 billion and had directly increased unemployment by about one percentage point.[77] "Higher oil prices had directly added 3.5 percent to the consumption price deflator and were projected to add roughly that much again through wage-price spiral effects.[78]

Phase IV was established on July 18, 1973.[79] It aimed at minimizing the secondary effects of the enormous increases in the prices of raw materials that had occurred during Phase III. Just as Phase II was designed to permit a gradual withdrawal from controls, Phase IV was designed to permit gradual elimination of the meat ceiling and the second freeze. Unlike Phase III's across the board approach, Phase IV decontrol strategy called for a sector by sector approach.[80]

The separate treatment of different sectors was designed in recognition of the enormous differential cost-pressures working their way through the economic system due to price increases of primary materials and imports. The regulations were intended to spread the expected consumer goods price increases over a longer period of time and generally to dampen price rises without disrupting supply.

John T. Dunlop, who oversaw Phase IV as head of the Cost of Living Council, described the Phase IV purpose and methodology as follows:

> Phase IV was also designed as a way out of controls, a purpose which the self-administration of Phase III had not achieved. The elimination of controls was to be achieved by lifting wage and price controls simultaneously on a sector by sector basis. Starting with the fertilizer industry in October and the cement industry in November, decontrol was granted in exchange for various commitments made by companies to limit price increases even beyond the expected expiration of control authority on April 30, 1974, to limit exports, to increase productive capacity, start up shut-down facilities, provide additional statistical data, and take various industrial relations steps in a few cases in cooperation with the collective bargaining agent. In general, decontrol prior to April 30, 1974 was to be achieved by a sector in exchange for commitments to restrain price and to increase supply.[81]

Presidential authority to impose a system of mandatory wage and price controls contained in the Economic Stabilization Act of 1970 expired at midnight on April 30, 1974.[82] By mid–June, the Cost of Living Council, left with only its monitoring function, had closed up shop.[83]

In the months that followed, double-digit inflation continued unchecked. The Consumer Price Index increased at an annual rate of 12.6 percent over those months.[84] The annual rate of increase in the Wholesale Price Index was an astounding 44 percent in July 1974, and more than 55 percent at a compound annual rate.[85]

The Ford Council on Wage and Price Stability

Government attention to the economy, as with other policy matters, was minimal during the summer of 1974 preceding the resignation of President Nixon. In his first speech to Congress, President Ford endorsed a bill establishing an executive group to monitor inflationary developments.[86] The bill was enacted within a matter of days.[87] It established the Council on Wage and Price Stability (COWPS), an eight-member board appointed by the president and charged with the task of monitoring the economy. The council, however, was a body with severely limited powers: it was expressly not authorized to impose mandatory economic controls;[88] it had no power to compel the production of cost, wage, price, or other information from the businesses which it was charged with monitoring; it could not compel production of profit or expense information from the IRS or other federal agencies;[89] it could not disclose cost information that it did receive from business or government agencies;[90] it was not given authority to use government purchasing power to resist inflationary price increases; it had a minimal budget and staff;[91] and its authorization lasted for only a year.[92]

Inflation continued unabated from March 1974 to March 1975. The Wholesale Price Index increased 12.5 percent (down from 18.8 percent for April 1973 to April 1974). The Consumer Price Index increased 10.3 percent from March 1974 to March 1975 (slightly higher than the figure for March 1973 to March 1974 of 10.2 percent.)[93]

COWPS efforts, consistent with its limited authority, were hortatory. For example, on November 25, 1974, it held public hearings to discuss the sharp increase in the price of sugar that had taken place. COWPS worked with food processors and the press to encourage sugar conservation and the promotion of sugar-free products.[94] The price of sugar fell, but COWPS action probably contributed little if anything to the decline. In December 1974, COWPS investigated price increases announced by three major steel producers. Albert Rees, Chairman of COWPS, stated that he was successful in achieving a 20 percent rollback in these prices, but it is unclear whether these companies initially asked for 125 percent (or more) of the price increases they wanted, anticipating the 20 percent rollbacks.[95]

S.409—The Senate Banking Committee COWPS Amendments of 1975

Dissatisfaction with the continuing high levels of inflation led to movement within the Senate Banking Committee to amend the 1974 Anti-Inflation Act to give COWPS some "teeth," that is, power to limit or delay price and wage increases.[96] Senate Bill 409, as originally proposed by Senators Proxmire and Stevenson, gave COWPS power "to require periodic reports" and to subpoena "books, papers and other documents relating to wages, prices, costs, profits and productivity by product line...."[97] COWPS was required to make available to the public any information collected from private firms unless the council determined that public disclosure of such information would "impose an undue competitive disadvantage" on the firms submitting the information[98] The bill authorized COWPS to require prenotification of wage and price increases by major companies and employee groups,[99] and also to delay inflationary price increases for up to sixty days.[100] Its budget was to be increased from $1 million to $4 million,[101] and its life was to be extended by two years to September 30, 1977.[102]

As enacted, S. 409 gave COWPS slightly sharper eyesight but no teeth. It authorized COWPS, for any purpose related to the Act, to:

> (1) require periodic reports for the submission of information maintained in the ordinary course of business; and (2) issue subpoenas signed by the Chairman or the Director for the attendance and testimony of witnesses and the production of relevant books, papers, and other documents, only to entities whose annual gross revenues are in excess of $5,000,000; relating to wages, costs, productivity, prices, sales, profits, imports and exports by product line or by such other categories as the Council may prescribe,[103]

It gave the Council authority to intervene in rule making and other proceedings before federal agencies to express its views as to the inflationary impact that might result from such proceedings.[104] It extended the life of the Council to September 30, 1977, as had been originally proposed,[105] and increased its budget from $1 million to $1.7 million.[106]

It is worth noting the difference between the informational burdens placed on businesses by the Proxmire-Stevenson bill and by the law as enacted.

First, although both drafts authorize the Council to subpoena books and other documents relating to wages, prices, costs, and so forth, by product line, the law as enacted limits this power to business and unions with annual gross revenues exceeding $5 million.

Second, although both drafts apparently authorize COWPS to require periodic reports relating to wages, prices, costs, and the like by product line (without a lower limit on the size of business or union which may be required to submit such a report), the law as enacted shifted a significant administrative burden onto COWPS. That is, under the Proxmire-Stevenson draft COWPS could require periodic reports without the restriction contained in the law as enacted that they be limited to "information maintained in the ordinary course of business." Under the Proxmire-Stevenson draft, COWPS could require any company to incur the expense of preparing a report on wages, prices, costs, profit, and productivity on a product-by-product basis, even if, as is thought to be the usual case, the company does not maintain such data on a product-by-product basis. Under the law as enacted, if the company does not maintain that information "in the ordinary course of business," or if its gross revenues are $5 million or less, COWPS was left in the dark. This raises an interesting and potentially important question. Suppose a company that presently does not maintain such information is required to maintain it at some point in the near future in order to comply with FTC Line of Business reporting requirements. Is maintenance of the data in order to meet FTC requirements then "in the ordinary course of business" for the purposes of this act?

Even if the size of the business is large enough to permit a subpoena to issue, the company need only turn over a mass of raw data. COWPS had to then sift through it, correlate it, and, with limited knowledge about how the company or industry works, devise some rule of thumb for allocating joint costs among the products of a multiproduct firm. Considering that COWPS had fewer than 50 people on its staff, the shift in administrative burden accomplished by this slight change in language was dispositive.

A third major difference between S. 409 as proposed and as enacted is that the draft required COWPS to disclose information submitted to it that would not impose a "competitive disadvantage on the firms submitting it,"[107] while the final legislation expressly prohibited the Council from disclosing product line information.[108] Furthermore, periodic reports to COWPS were made immune from legal process.[109]

During 1975, the Consumer Price Index's upward movement decelerated a bit but toward the year's end was still increasing at a distressing 8.4 percent per year.[110] Food and fuel prices continued to be a major problem.[111] Inflation in services' prices continued at 6 percent per year—no faster than in 1974. But medical costs rose at a rate of 1 percent *per month* in 1975.[112] Following enactment of the 1975 amendments, COWPS engaged in efforts to assess the inflationary impact of new government regulations.[113] It challenged regulatory proposals across a broad spectrum of health, safety, and environmental topics—airport noise, shellfish, truck and bus brakes, design of tanker bottoms, Amtrak passenger routes, vinyl chloride in food packaging, lawn mower safety, and motorcycle emissions.[114]

Some critics alleged that these efforts were antiregulatory but not necessarily anti-inflationary.[115] Even taken on its own terms, COWPS's analysis has been faulted on numerous grounds.[116] COWPS reportedly operated on the assumption that if the costs of the regulation do not outweigh its benefits (express or imputed), then the regulation is inflationary. Consumer Product Safety Commission economist Walter J. Prunella has argued that the legislative history of the 1972 Consumer Product Safety Act indicates that Congress did not want a cost-benefit analysis done.[117] Regardless of whether or not Mr. Prunella is correct in his reading of legislative history, it is clear that COWPS policy was grounded upon a different operating assumption.[118] COWPS's assumption results from a confusion of relative price changes (which must occur in noninflationary as well as inflationary times to achieve efficient resource allocation) with changes in the absolute price level (true inflation). To take the simplest case, suppose the regulation confers no benefit. The firm's cost of compliance with the regulation will be similar to a per unit excise tax. The price of the regulated good will increase to the extent that this tax is shifted onto consumers of the good. The extent of shifting depends on the market power of the firm, which in turn depends in large part on the availability of close substitutes, the prices of which have decreased relative to the price of the regulated goods.[119] Whatever increase occurs in the price of the regulated good, its inflationary impact depends on the good's importance in the consumer budgets and the availability of substitutes.

Secondly, the assumption in no small way hinged on COWPS's ability to resolve very tricky definitional problems. Suppose private benefits of the regulation exceed private costs (compliance) but public plus private benefits fall short of public plus private costs (administrative plus compliance). What resolution? Moreover, if costs and benefits occur over time, what discount rate should be used to reduce these flows to present value? A private-market rate of return? A social-time preference rate? How is the latter chosen?[120] Clear counterexamples to COWPS' assumption are cases where the real dollar benefits exceed the real dollar costs of a regulation but imputed adverse side-effects (that are not recognized by the private market) increase total costs such that they exceed benefits. In such a case, imposition of the regulation would not be inflationary as defined by the private-market since the dollar increase in value of the regulated good exceeds the dollar increment in cost.

Finally, simple comparisons of dollar benefits with dollar costs contain implicit assumptions about the constancy of, or changes in, the marginal utility of money to different consumers as the regulation is imposed. That is, COWPS must assume that the marginal utility of money to all individuals with respect to regulation of all commodities is unchanged or always is changed by the same amount when any regulation is imposed. There is no foundation for this assumption.[121] For all these reasons COWPS' approach to this problem was at one and the same time too simplistic and too reliant on subjective choice of determinative parameters. A *New York Times* report on COWPS observed:

> One view within the administration is that although the council does good analysis, its scatter-shot method of going after what it sees as a few flagrant examples of unjustified regulatory proposals represents a misallocation of resources. In this view, the council has little over-all inhibiting effect.
>
> Alternatively, it is said the resources could be better used if they were devoted to a single problem regulatory area or agency....[122]

The Carter Council on Wage and Price Stability

When President Carter took office, the Consumer Price Index and prime rate were each about 6 percent. As these rose toward 9 percent in October 1978, the president announced an anti-inflation program that included voluntary pay and price standards.[123]

Although compliance with the voluntary guidelines was not universal, they effectively restrained two key prices: industrial-price increases (which inflated at a rate of between 7.5 and 10 percent by the end of 1979) and employment costs (which inflated at a 7 to 9 percent rate and actually decelerated when compared with comparable prior figures).[124] The conclusion is inescapable that industrial prices are easier to hold down than other prices because industrial business units are large, publicly visible, and relatively concentrated. The guidelines shifted industrial administered pricing from a purely private to public-private exercise.[125] On the other hand, wages have universally been recognized as relatively easier to control than even industrial prices (incentives of business after all are on the same side as government here).[126]

The Carter Administration was sharply, and accurately, criticized by organized labor precisely because wage pacts lagged 2 to 5 percentage points behind the CPI during 1978–1979 as companies enforced the pay guidelines while less conscientiously following price norms.

In fairness to COWPS, the wage picture under the guidelines was not all that simple. In fact, there was a wide variation in the magnitude of pay increases. Some of the variation can be traced to the effects of contracts negotiated before the guidelines program. But in addition, pay-rate increases varied substantially among employee units that complied due to the many exemptions to the general pay standard. The most troublesome variations reflect the preferential treatment of employee units covered by cost-of-living-adjustment clauses (COLAs) as contrasted with typically less powerful employee groups not so covered. COLAs were factored into the guidelines at an arbitrarily low cost of 6 percent. Consequently, workers with a pay increase of 7 percent and those with a 1 percent increase plus a cost-of-living adjustment were both deemed to be within a 7 percent pay limit, but the latter got full protection against 1979's 12 percent inflation while the former did not.[127]

Carter's unsuccessful real-wage insurance proposal was an attempt to use tax incentives to moderate wage claims by allowing a tax credit equal to the difference between a prejudicially moderate wage settlement and COWPS's target for average wage settlements, 7 percent.[128] It stalled in Congress and was abandoned.

According to COWPS, the above-mentioned moderation of wage-increases, achieved even without real-wage insurance but subject to great variation, was offset by "dismal productivity performance."[129] A 1.3 percent *fall* in output per man-hour between October 1978 and November 1979, together with the 8.8 percent rise in total labor compensation (including social security tax increases), resulted in a 10.2 percent increase in unit labor costs.[130] "The productivity collapse, the large increase in social security taxes, and the explosion in energy prices resulted in a significant decline in average real earnings."[131]

A closer look at this performance of the Carter guidelines, as summarized by COWPS's own Inflation Update and Issue Papers, demonstrates COWPS's own recognition of the limits of the guidelines and the need for an alternative to the policy of "muddle-through". COWPS's *Inflation Update* begins with a summary that the attentive reader should find hauntingly reminiscent of the Nixon approach:

> During the past year, the inflation rate accelerated to double-digit levels. Yet much of this acceleration is attributable to factors that were not and could not have been controlled by this or any other anti-inflation program. In those areas where the price and pay standards were directly applicable, the aggregate data suggest that these standards—by preventing the food and fuel price explosion from being built into the industrial wage and price structure—have kept a very bad situation from being appreciably worse.[132]

In other words inflation in food prices, energy prices and housing prices was "beyond the reach of the [guidelines] program."[133] If so, Americans might well demand what necessities of life are left? The National Center for Economic Alternatives has identified one other necessity—health care—but, unfortunately, it was *not* covered by the program either and the COWPS reports ignore it. Health care costs inflated at an annual rate of about 10 percent through the 1970s.

If "muddling-through" means anything it means failure to learn from recent experience, and failure to adapt systematically to the unexpected. Both characterized the Carter guidelines. Energy, food, housing, and health were the nemesis ot the Nixon program; Carter also largely ignored the key sectors. Second, Carter didn't adapt when his prediction proved wrong. At the time the guidelines program was announced, most economic forecasters were predicting a recession by early 1979. "These anticipations should be borne in mind because pay and price standards can also be expected to be most effective in moderating wage and price increases in an economy characterized by slack rather than tight market conditions."[134] The Federal Reserve was also expected to relax its monetary policy somewhat, reversing a two-year climb in interest rates.[135] The Department of Agriculture predicted 7 percent food price inflation assuming an average winter.[136] Finally, following three straight years of moderate OPEC pricing, a fourth straight year was expected—or hoped for.[137] "All of these expectations proved incorrect."[138] COWPS did not react. But worse still, Carter, not to be accused of benign neglect, decontrolled "old" domestic crude oil on June 1, 1979, [139] and, through his new Federal Reserve Chairman, sent the prime above 16 percent on October 6.

As the *Inflation Update* noted,

> The economic parallels between 1973–1975 and the current period are deeply disturbing. The earlier period was characterized by a similar explosion in food and energy prices, which eventually worked their way into

the underlying rate of inflation... If economic history were to repeat itself, a sharp increase in the underlying rate—well into double-digit levels—could be expected about now.[140]

This time, COWPS's expectations were fullfilled. Inflation in 1980 hit a sustained rate of 20 percent and averaged out to an annualized rate of over 12 percent for the year.

Reagan—The Watchdog Is Put to Sleep

One of Ronald Reagan's first acts as president was to demobilize and disband the Council on Wage and Price Stability. Thus, the inflation "watchdog," toothless from birth and blind and deaf under Ford and Carter, was put to sleep. It was just as well. No one had ever heard it bark, and everyone knew it couldn't bite.

The Classical Criticisms of Controls—And A Response

Mandatory wage and price controls are a bit like Amtrak. Almost every criticism you have ever heard about either is probably at least partially correct. And neither was ever meant to be a permanent government endeavor. Yet—and this is often overlooked—each can be made to work effectively for a temporary period, thereby carrying the nation across bumpy natural or economic terrain at a lower social cost than if the private market were left to its own course. This section reviews the considerable shortcomings of direct anti-inflationary programs, particularly mandatory controls, in light of the experience of World War II, Korean War, Kennedy, Nixon, Ford, Carter, and Reagan efforts. These shortcomings include high administrative cost, ineffectiveness, waste, procedural unfairness, complexity, delay, unresponsiveness of the bureaucratic machinery to democratic control, inherent unpredictability of the wage-price results in many cases, and uneven impact on income distribution. Discussion of several of these shortcomings will be grouped around three principal themes: (1) controls require a huge bureaucracy; (2) they lead to shortages (undesirable from an allocative point of view and indicative of the redistributional effects of controls); and (3) they are self-defeating since a price explosion inevitably follows decontrol.

Administering Controls—Public and Private
Bureaucracy

Mention of controls typically conjures up the image of thousands of bureaucrats arbitrarily dictating prices for millions of goods and services. In fact, the actual record is much less dreadful than this image. At the peak of World War II controls, there were only one thousand investigators enforcing food price and rationing regulations at all levels of production and marketing.[141] No doubt wartime morale eased the enforcement task, and the small public bureaucracy was accompanied by a much larger private bureaucratic burden. One firm estimated that, during the Korean War controls program, it had to process one million purchase orders and invoices to comply with regulatory record keeping for controlled prices. Another spent over twenty-one thousand hours on compliance matters.[142] And the final report of the Council on Wage and Price Stability estimated the administrative costs imposed by the Carter program to have been less than $10 million annually for COWPS' budget and $300 million annually for the private sector's cost of compliance.[143] Estimates of the total public and private costs of compliance with mandatory controls in the mid 1980s, based on the Nixon-program experience, would range from $1 billion to $4 billion.[144]

Yet such costs do not assure compliance. During the 90-day price freeze of 1971, for example, over forty-six thousand violations were reported to the government, and there must certainly have been many unreported violations.[145] Controls, therefore, depend considerably on voluntary compliance, public pressure, and the use of self-executing rules subject to prior government approval or government revocation. As will be discussed, each of these factors is strongest at the outset of the controls program and weakens over time.

Still, the public and private administrative costs of controls are very low indeed when compared with the value of lost national product resulting from allowing (or facilitating) a recession in order to slow the new inflation. According to a Congressional Budget Office Study, the cost of even a mild recession (with 1 percent increase in unemployment) is a staggering $47 billion in lost GNP for each 1 percent reduction in the inflation rate.[146] Arthur Okun estimated the cost to be four times that figure.

Methodology and Side Effects—Cost Increases,
Pseudoinnovation, Stifled Investment, and Shortages

Only one basic method has been devised that permits the government to control the prices of thousands of products and services while avoiding the impossible task of a firm-by-firm determination of prices based on the costs of goods sold or of services rendered. That method is a base-price system, typically grounded on the highest price charged during a "base period," such as the month prior to an initial freeze.[147]

A base-period wage-price control scheme avoids the problem, which would lead to immediate breakdown of the program, of determining first the individual cost of thousands of products and services and then an allowable mark-up above cost for each. The government, not to mention individual firms, simply has no idea what those costs are. Consequently, use of prices charged during a base period as a point of reference is the only verifiable marker available to the government.[148] Despite many difficulties, the historical-price method of administering controls is administratively simple. Historical prices are usually ascertainable, cost increases above the base period can usually be determined by producers relatively easily, the historical-price rule can apply to all industry, and it is a rule that is readily understood and largely self-enforceable.[149] These advantages are particularly strong at the outset of the controls program. However, even as the historical-price rule shifts into a rule of historical price *plus* allowable cost increases, as it must in certain cases, much of the administrative simplicity remains.

Pure historically based pricing, that is, a freeze, is practical for a very short time only. A competitive economic system, even one with a large degree of concentration and government participation, is in a perpetual process of equilibrium adjustment. Its ordered perpetual motion has been compared to a dance: the scene constantly changing, participants constantly entering, leaving, and changing relationships, some moving smoothly, some not.[150] A freeze catches some participants in awkward positions (seasonally low or high prices, goods being sold at low "introductory"prices, purely customized producers whose next product does not resemble their last) and, therefore, creates inequities. Exceptions must be made, and some uncontrollable cost increases must be allowed to be passed through to consumers. The dance is no longer frozen still as if captured by a stop-action camera. Instead, some participants are allowed to make certain adjustments. There is some movement, but it is wooden, not the smooth, creative flow that exists when individuals are left to decide for themselves.

Typically, a freeze shifts to a system combining historical price and certain allowable costs as some sellers are squeezed between uncontrollable cost increases and frozen prices. For example, real property, newspapers, common carriers, insurance, and professional fees were exempted from control by the Korean War price-control legislation. In that period, and again during the Nixon controls program, raw agricultural commodities were exempted primarily because of the volatility of their prices due to weather changes and perishability. As prices rose for exempt commodities, costs rose for producers using them as inputs.[151]

Over time, one exemption either leads to another (for those using exempted items as inputs) or to cost-pass-through allowances. Refusal to permit downstream exemption or cost pass throughs would result in unfairness and withdrawal or quality deterioration of downstream products. Allowing some dancers to move, even woodenly, will lead to their bumping into dancers still frozen still. The latter will either topple like bowling pins or, if allowed to move, move stiffly across the dance floor, eventually bumping into others. In World War II, such cost squeezes *eventually* led manufacturers to produce "sports shirts but not white shirts, three-inch boards but not one-inch boards, apple jelly with sugar, but not sugar alone.[152]

Output substitution, deterioration of quality, and other behavioral effects characteristic of planned economies inevitably arise. For example, allowance of certain cost increases encourages manufacturers to add to cost, since the greater the total cost, the greater will be total profit at a given profit margin. Similarly, pseudoinnovation is encouraged if prices of new products are less tightly controlled than were those in the base period, since the new product's price must be set equal to some comparable base-period product or calculated with allowable total costs. Conversely, price (and, implicitly, profit) control discourages both new investment and true innovation if the financial rewards of making improvements cannot be captured by the investor or innovator.[153].

Over the short run, there are ways to cope with several of these problems that have been tried in the past. During World War II, the Office of Price Administration (OPA) permitted some firms, such as grocery stores, to set prices based on costs plus a formula mark-up.[154] Where technological innovation is not a prominent aspect of an industry's growth and where competition prevails (probably true of supermarketing in most areas of the country in the 1970s and 1980s), a cost-plus-fixed-margin formula is workable during a controls period. Such a formula method has been applied to many industries, supplemented by special authorizations to raise price.[155] In the Korean War program, raw-agricultural-price increases, certain transportation costs, and, later, import costs were allowed to be passed through.[156] Eventually numerous "pass through" standards were developed for individual industries or firms.[157] During the Nixon program, as noted earlier in this chapter, after the initial 90-day freeze, manufacturers and retailers were permitted to pass through allowable cost increases subject to a maximum profit ceiling.[158]

Recognition that certain allowable cost increases must eventually pass through the system creates the tension, characteristic of an effective controls program, between centralized rule-making delay on the one hand and delegation on the other. Even if certain cost pass throughs are allowed in order to avert serious shortages or to encourage new investment, the bureaucratic process delays implementation of pass-through allowance, because of both deliberate and unintentional reasons, unless pass-through applications are self-executing. In other words, delay furthers the purpose of price restraint up to a point short of severe shortage. Consequently, wage-price regulators choose procedures that build in some delay. Indeed, one senior price regulator, who did not want to be quoted, told this author that the ability to delay cost pass throughs is the key control power.

Obviously, the problem is a very delicate one since government review of cost-pass-through applications from individual firms takes considerable time, even if the government has not decided that delay is warranted and unlikely to lead to shortage. The regulator's decision to delay must take such inherent lags into account or risk prolonging price increases longer than intended, resulting in shortages.[159]

At the risk of undercutting the control effort's effectiveness, delay can be overcome by allowing firms to make their own price adjustments. During the Korean War, a trend developed to permit small businesses to automatically adjust prices after a waiting period subject to OPS review and readjustment.[160] During Phases II and III of the Nixon program, firms with less than $100 million in sales were permitted to make automatic price adjustments, but firms above that threshold had to obtain prior approval.[161]

The discussion thus far begs one of the most difficult questions: the determination, through the use of general standards, of when a firm is justfied in passing through costs.[162] This is the problem of classification—classifying certain types of cost increases as allowable over scheduled time periods. This often entails tricky judgments about allowable profit levels, since a profit-level ceiling is often a stipulated condition of cost allowance, as it was in the Nixon program. Misclassification can lead to silly results, such as different prices for the same product. In World War II, it was dicovered that pillow feathers from "live" chickens (an uncontrolled agricultural good) differed from those made from dead chickens (a controlled industrial good).[163] Conversely, failure to distinguish real differences between products and associated costs (and to classify them differently) can lead to shortage and inequity. Yet pressure to increase the number of distinctions leads to a proliferation of rules and classifications. The advantage of fairly clear general principles and avoidance of case-by-case determination is not sustainable indefinitely. As one of the World War II regulators wrote of the historically based method:

> [I]ts maximum utility was achieved at the moment it was imposed and its utility diminished steadily as the time span since the base period increased. Inevitably, there were new products, new sellers, new types of buyers, new selling areas, new conditions of sales, new volume conditions, new container types and sizes. Experience showed that to meet such problems the freeze approach, even when strengthened by the use of price bridges, had to be supplemented by other and more flexible techniques.[164]

Those techniques were based on allowable costs.[165]

Will a Price Explosion Follow?

The price explosion following decontrol of prices in the Nixon program and similar phenomena following the World War II and Korean War programs has quite understandably, led many commentators to conclude that any short-run slowdown of inflation during controls is more than compensated for during the period that follows as the freed market exacts its penalty for product and capital shortages created by controls.[166] One authoritative scholar has argued that serious controls, which attempt to keep prices well below market clearing levels, can only be successful if accompanied by rationing.[167] Otherwise, a black market will develop—indeed, it may develop despite a combination of controls plus rationing. And the black-market prices would be the harbingers of dramatic market-price increases following decontrol.[168]

The new inflation is being pushed along by jolts in food and energy costs that would at best be bottled up temporarily by controls and would return with decontrol. The concern about a post-control price explosion is a legitimate one, so weighty, in fact, that a short-term freeze-and-phase controls program ought not be attempted unless it is accompanied by implementation of long-run reforms aimed at the key supply issues that cause the new inflation. In other words, mandatory controls can be less painful than recession and could form a transitional phase pending implementation of long-run targeted policies in food, housing, energy, and health—the supply bottlenecks that would fuel the postcontrol inflation just as they fuel the present inflation.

The choice between implementing controls and implementing the sectoral reforms discussed elsewhere in this book is clear. Controls are not needed as a prelude to those reforms. Any argument for controls is predicated on their preferability to recession as a temporary antidote to inflation. However, sectoral reforms are a necessary complement to controls, since the aftershock of controls could be reduced in proportion to such reforms. Specifically, management of our grain exports could be coordinated with decontrol so that domestic supplies of feed grains for livestock and cereals were disproportionately high. Conservation and solar and synthetic energy development could be coordinated with gasoline rationing (by coupon or tax) so that increases in the former necessitated less rationing at a given level of national oil imports. To some extent, controls and allocation of credit toward mortgage lending would assist the housing sector in a more than temporary way, since the recession has especially long-run impact on the many small firms making up that industry. And hospital-cost containment would continue a form of cost control in the health sector.

Notes

1. The classic works on economic stabilization are those of J.K. Galbraith: "Reflections on Price Control," *Quarterly Journal of Eco-*

nomics, August, 1946; "The Disequilibrium System," *American Economic Review,* June, 1947; "Market Structure and Stabilization Policy," *Review of Economic Statistics,* May, 1957; and his book *A Theory of Price Control,* Cambridge, Harvard University Press (1952). Other helpful references are: Bronfenbrenner and Holzman, Survey of Inflation Theory, 53 *Am. Econ. Rev* 646–652 (1963); Seymour Harris, *Price and Related Controls in the United States* (N.Y.: McGraw Hill, 1945); Harvey Mansfield, *A Short History of OPA* (Washington: Office of Price Administration, 1947). F. Scherer, *Industrial Market Structure and Economic Performance* 288, 410–416 (1971); Barry Bosworth, statement before the Subcommittee on Economic Stabilization of the Committee on Banking, Housing, and Urban Affairs, February 1, 1980.

2. See, for example, Henry Aaron, "Taxation and Inflation," Report on Brookings Conference on Taxation and Inflation (1976). Joseph Minarik's static analysis of inflation as a tax on wealth does not refute the statement made in the text. It should be clear that those with greater wealth and power at any given point in time will, on average, have greater ability to protect it from inflation's grip through shifting investment portfolios or raising prices for their services. See *Inflation in the Necessities,* Brookings Bulletin, 1980.

Lester Thurow has observed that, from 1972 to 1978, despite inflation, real per capita disposable income rose 16 percent across all income classes (See *Challenge,* March–April 1980). Although this suggests that there were no shifts in the distribution of income, it does not indicate that there were no shifts in the standard of living over those years. The burden of the argument here is to show that inflation in the necessities (food, energy, housing, and health) proceeded at a much more rapid rate than other inflation. Consequently, the standard of living of lower-income groups, who spend a far higher percentage of their incomes on necessities, declined relative to the average. Moreover, there has been continuing severe inflation coupled with a severe recession since 1978, as Thurow himself points out.

Minarik and Thurow are more fully answered in appendix A.

3. Statement by Barry Bosworth before the Subcommittee on Economic Stabilization of the Committee on Banking, Housing, and Urban Affairs, February 1, 1980, at 16.

4. For a discussion of anti-inflation policy from 1945 to 1961, see: *Exhortation and Controls: The Search for a Wage-Price Policy 1945-71,* 9–134 (C. Goodwin, ed., 1975).

5. M. Evans, *Macroeconomic Activity, Theory, Forecasting, and Control, Harper and Row, New York,* at 540 (1969).

6. See *Exhortation and Controls: The Search for a Wage-Price Policy 1945-1971,* Brookings Institution, Washington, D.C., 149–154, 190–191. (C.Goodwin, ed. 1975).

7. M. Evans, *supra,* note 5, at 540.

8. Id. at 541.

9. Id.

10. Id.

11. Id.

12. U.S. Bureau of Labor Statistics, Dept. of Labor, Handbook of Labor Statistics 276 (1972).

13. *Exhortation And Controls: The Search For A Wage-Price Policy 1945-1971,* 295 (C. Goodwin, ed. 1975).

14. The Economic Stabilization Act of 1970, P. L. No. 91-379, 84 Stat. 799 (1970) was originally enacted as part of an amendment to the Defense Production Act of 1950, which President Nixon did not want to veto. The act was then expanded and extended to April 30, 1972, P. L. No. 92-15, 85 Stat. (1971). Subsequent revisions for two one-year periods finally expired on April 30, 1974. P. L. No. 92-210, 85 Stat. 743 (1971), P.L. No, 93-28 Stat. 27 (1973).

15. J. Dunlop, "Inflation and Income Policies: The Political Economy of Recent U.S. Experience," 5, Oct. 19, 1974 (unpublished Harvard Economics Seminar Memorandum).

16. Exec. Order No. 11588, 36 Fed. Reg. 6339 (1971).

17. Dunlop, *supra,* note 15, at 6.

18. A. Weber, *In Pursuit of Price Stability: The Wage-Price Freeze of 1971,* Brookings Institution, Washington, D.C.,1 (1973).

19. See: Office of Economic Stabilization of the Department of the Treasury, *Historical Working Papers on the Economic Stabilization Program, August 15, 1971 to April 30, 1974,* at 9-10 (1974) (hereafter cited as *Historical Working Papers).*

The Historical Working Papers comprise 2348 pages of published description and anlysis of most aspects of the administration of the Economic Stabilization Program. Importantly, however, food price policy and behavior is not included in the published study. It is suggested that food was too "controversial" an area to be treated in an official report. *Historical Working Papers,* 1425. More likely, the omission is due to the Nixon Administration's understandable reticence to publicize the failure of its food inflation policies. The *Historical Working Papers* make reference to two unpublished studies prepared for the Office of Economic Stabilization and filed in the National Archives: G. Nelson, "Food and Agricultural Policy in 1971-74, Reflections on Controls and Their Impact", December 1974 (National Archives Record Group No. 432, Box 956, 197 pages), and R. Brown, "Regulating Food Prices During the Economic Stabilization Program 1971-74", December 1974 (National Archives Record Group No. 432, Box 956, 76 pages). The latter is a thoughtful and sharply critical essay on the Economic Stabilization Program's approach to control of food price inflation. It is curiously marked "Not Published—Only Copy. SE-QUESTERED." Perhaps it was thought too critical for general distribution. Certain aspects of the Nelson and Brown studies were published in *The Lessons of Wage and Price Controls — The Food Sector,* Harvard Univercity Press (1977) especially Chapter I and V. See also A. Weber, *supra,* note 10, which evaluates Phase I.

20. See *Historical Working Papers,* at 9–10.

21. Id.

22. Dunlop, *supra,* note 15, at 6.

23. Exec. order No. 11615, 36 Fed. Reg. 15727 (1971), 12 U.S.C. § 1904 (Supp. III, 1973), issued under authority of the Economic Stabilization Act of 1970, P.L. No. 91–379, § 203, 84 Stat. 799 (1979).

24. The Council comprised the Secretaries of the Treasury, Agriculture, Commerce, Labor, and Housing and Urban Development (the latter was not named in Exec. Order No. 11615, but was included in the amending Exec. Order No. 11617, 36 Fed. Reg. 17813 (1971)); the Director of the Office of Management and Budget, the Chairman of the Council of Economic Advisors; the Director of the Office of Emergency Preparedness; the Special Assistant to the President for Consumer Affairs; and, as advisor, the chairman of the Federal Reserve Board.

25. For a survey of the policy planning of Phase I, see *Historical Working Papers, supra,* note 19, at 8–20.

26. A. Weber, *supra,* note 18, at 100.

27. Id.

28. Id. at 101

29. Id. at 122.

30. G. Nelson, *supra,* note 19, at 33.

31. Id., R. Brown, *supra,* note 19, at 4.

32. A. Weber, *supra,* note 18, at 126–127.

33. Economic Report of the President 57,228 (January 1973).

34. Exec. Order No. 11627, 36 Fed. Reg. 20139 (1971).

35. R. Lanzillotti, M. Hamilton and R. Roberts, Phase II in Review: The Price Commission Experience, Brookings Institution, Washington, D.C., 1 (1975).

36. See *Historical Working Papers, supra,* note 19, at 116, 118.

37. *Historical Working Papers, supra,* note 19, at 22–26, 116. See also, R. Lanzillotti, *supra,* note 33, at 9–26. Presidential authority underpinning Phase II was strengthened by the Economic Stabilization Act Amendments of 1972, P. L. No. 92–210, 85 Stat. 743 (1971).

38. Economic Report of the President 96–100 (January 1972). See, generally, *Guidelines, Informed Controls, and the Market Place: Policy Choices in a Full Employment Economy* (G. Shultz, R. Aliber, eds. 1966). See, also, J. Sheehan, *The Wage Price Guideposts* (1967).

39. R. Lanzillotti, *supra,* note 35, at 34–35.

40. J. Dunlop, *supra,* note 15, at 7.

41. G. Nelson, *supra,* note 19, at 38.

42. R. Brown, *supra,* note 19, at 5.

43. Id.

44. 36 Fed. Reg. 21790 (1971).

45. R. Brown, *supra,* note 19, at 7.

46. G. Nelson, *supra,* note 19, at 51–52.

47. Id. at 51, 53.

48. Albright, "Some Deal," *N. Y. Times,* Nov. 26, 1973 (Magazine), at 95, Col. 2. See also Hathaway, Food Prices and Inflation," Brookings Papers on Economic Activity, 63, 85–90 (1974); J. Schnittker, "The 1972–73 Food Price Spiral," Brookings Papers on Economic Activity, 498–506 (1973).

49. U.S. Dept. of Agriculture, Wheat Situation, WS-221, August 1972 at 3.

50. Albright, *supra,* note 48, at 95, col. 3.

51. G. Nelson, *supra,* note 19, at 54.

52. Id.

53. G. Nelson, *supra,* note 19, at 55.

54. *Id.* at 55.

55. U.S. Dept. of Agriculture, *supra,* note 49, at 9–10.

56. R. Lanzillotti, *supra,* note 35, at 114.

57. These statistics, published by the President's Council of Economic Advisers, were obtained from Hal Weisman, Member, Office of Price Policy, Price Commission, and from Interstate and Foreign Commerce Committee Report on Hospital Cost Containment (1977) at 4; and American Hospital Association Hospital Statistics (1979) at v.

58. Exec. Order No. 11695, 6 C.F.R. 605 (1974) 12 U.S.C. § 1904 (supp. III, 1973).

59. *Historical Working Papers, supra,* note 19, at 138.

60. 6 C.F.R. § 130.13 (1974)

61. R. Lanzillotti, *supra,* note 35, at 139.

62. J. Dunlop, *supra,* note 15, at 9.

63. R. Brown, *supra,* note 19, at 9.

64. Id. at 9.

65. G. Nelson, *supra,* note 19, at 57–60, describes other inflationary decisions of the Department of Agriculture. For example, throughout 1972, the Department recommended a reduction in egg production in order to gain "improvement" in egg prices. These rose sharply from 55 cents per dozen at retail in November 1972 to 74 cents in January 1973. To make matters worse, in January the Department recommended a cutback in broiler production—at the very time when the prices of poultry and meat

(which are forms of processed grain) were skyrocketing in reaction to the Russian grain deal and other stimuli.

66. R. Lanzillotti, *supra,* note 35, at 198.

67. *Historical Working Papers, supra,* note 19, at 51.

68. Id. at 43.

69. Id. at 51–52. On April 30, 1973, the Economic Stabilization Act was extended until April 30, 1974. P. L. No. 93–28, 87 Stat. 27 (1973).

70. Brown, *supra,* note 19, at 11.

71. *Historical Working Papers, supra,* note 19, at 52–53.

72. Exec. Order No. 11723, 6 C.F.R. 612 (1974), 12 U.S.C. § 1904 (Supp. III, 1973).

73. *Historical Working Papers, supra,* note 19, at 161.

74. *Higher Oil Prices and the World Economy,* The Adjustment Problem 1–2, (E. Fried and C. Schultze, eds.), Brookings Institution, Washington, D. C. (1975).

75. Id.

76. Id. at 27.

77. Id. at 103.

78. Id.

79. Exec. Ord. No. 11730, July 18, 1973 Fed. Reg. 19345.

80. *Historical Working Papers, supra,* note 19, at 63.

81. J. Dunlop, *supra,* note 15, at 12. Reprinted with permission.

82. P. L. No. 91–379, 84 Stat. 799 (1970) (codified at 12 U.S.C. § 1904 (Supp. III, 1973)).

83. Exec. Order No. 11781, 39 Fed. Reg. 15749 (1974) provided for an "orderly transition" from mandatory controls. Exec. Order No. 11788, 39 Fed. Reg. 22113 (1974), abruptly killed the Council.

84. 121 Cong. Rec. 7545 (daily ed. May 6, 1975) (remarks of Senator Muskie).

85. Id.

86. 121 Cong. Rec. 8160 (daily ed. August 12, 1975).

87. Council on Wage and Price Stability Act of 1974, 12 U.S.C.A. § 1904 (Supp. 1980).

88. Id. § 3(b).

89. Id. § 4(e).

90. Id. § 4(b), (c), (d).

91. Id., §§ 2(b), (d), 6. The Council staff numbered about 35. Hearings on S. 409. Statement by Albert Rees, Director of the Council on Wage and Price Stability.

92. Id., § 7.

93. 121 Cong. Rec. 7545 (daily ed. May 6, 1975) (remarks of Senator Kennedy).

94. *Hearings on S. 409, supra,* note 1, at 13.

95. Id. Without power to subpoena cost information, COWPS could not be certain that the allowed price increase was justified by cost increases, but Mr. Rees stated that this "appeared" to be so.

96. Id. at 1-3.

97. Id. at 6.

98. Id. at 7.

99. Id.

100. Id. at 8.

101. Id. at 9.

102. Id. at 10.

103. P. L. No. 94-78 § 3 (Aug. 9, 1975).

104. Id. § 4.

105. Id. § 7.

106. Id. § 6.

107. *Hearings on S. 409, supra,* note 1, at 2-3.

108. P. L. No. 94-78 § 5(f) (1) (August 9, 1975).

109. Id. § 5 (f) (2).

110. U.S. Bureau of Labor Statistics, Department of Labor, CPI Detailed Report 1 (October 1975). Seasonally adjusted monthly rate was .7%; without adjustment, .6%.

111. Food prices rose 3.2% during June and July after rising only 1.5% during the first five months of 1975. Wholesale food prices from March through July rose 7% indicating that food price figures for the final quarter of 1975 would keep rising strongly. *Business Week,* September 8, 1975, at 15-16.

112. Id. at 16.

113. See Cowan, "One U.S. Agency Worries About Costs", *N.Y. Times,* January 11, 1975, § 3, at 2.

114. Id.

115. Id.

116. Id.

117. Id.

118. Id.

119. See: Scherer, *Industrial Market Structure and Economic Performance,* Rand McNally, Chicago, 288-290 (1971)

120. See: Millward, *Public Expenditure Economics,* McGraw Hill, London, 195-198 (1971).

121. Dougherty, Thomas, *The State of Thought about Consumers' Surplus,* Economic Theory Seminar, Oxford University, Michaelmas Term 1972 (unpublished essay).

122. Cowan, *supra,* note 113. Reprinted with permission.

123. Executive Order No. 12092, 3 C.F.R. 249 (1978). See also 44 Fed. Reg. 1229 (1979).

124. Council on Wage and Price Stability, Release 353, November 21, 1979, *Inflation Update* (hereinafter referred to as COWPS Inflation Update).

125. See F. Scherer, *Industrial Market Structure and Economic Performance,* (Chicago: Rand McNally) 288–290 (1971).

126. See, for example, J. Flemming, *Inflation,* London: Oxford University Press, 1976.

127. Council on Wage and Price Stability Issue Paper: Pay and Price Standards, August 7, 1979.

128. Daniel J.B. Mitchell, "Controlling Inflation" in *Setting National Priorities — The 1980 Budget,* Washington, D.C.: Brookings Institution (1980) at 84.

129. Inflation Update at 4.

130. Id.

131. Id.

132. Inflation Update at 1.

133. COWPS's August 7, 1979 Issue Paper at 1.

134. Inflation Update at 2.

135. Id.

136. Id.

137. Id.

138. Id.

139. Estimates of the impact of this decision on the U.S. economy by the staff of the House Committee on Interstate and Foreign Commerce include an *added* jolt of 4 percent to the inflation rate and an additional $1000 per family per year for home heating. (Discussion with staff). President Reagan acted immediately to phase in decontrol of "old" oil more rapidly.

140. Inflation Update, at 11.

141. T. Manning, *The Office of Price Administration,* (New York, 1960) at 18.

142. Chamber of Commerce of the United States, *The Price of Price Controls* (Washington, D.C. 1951) at 14–15.

143. Council on Wage and Price Stability, *"Evaluation of the Pay and Price Standards Program,"* Mimeograph, January 1981.

144. See Testimony of John T. Dunlop in *Oversight on Economic Stabilization,* Hearings before the Subcommittee on Production and Stabilization of the U.S. Senate Committee on Banking, Housing and Urban Affairs (Washington, D.C.: U.S. Government Printing Office, February 1974), Appendix P; *see also* Lanzillotti, et al., *Phase II in Review, The Price Commission Experience* (Washington, D.C.: Brookings Institution, 1975) at 192. By comparison, it is estimated that in 1977, forty-eight companies, accounting for 8 percent of nonagricultural sales, spent $2.6

billion to comply with all federal regulations (mostly environmental regulations). Arthur Anderson & Co., *Cost of Government Regulation, Study for The Business Roundtable* (March 1979).

145. A. Weber, *In Pursuit of Price Stability: The Wage-Price Freeze of 1971* (Washington, D.C.: Brookings Institution, 1973) at 106–111; *Stemming Inflation: The OEP and the Ninety Day Freeze* (Washington, D.C., 1972) at 121; Office of Emergency Preparedness, "Weekly Summary Report Nov. 2, 1971 through Close of Business Nov. 9, 1971." Spot checks during the Korean War indicated that possibly 25 to 50 percent of firms were in violation. A. Flory, "Field Administration in OPS," 19 *Law and Contemporary Problems* (1954): 604, 621.

146. Congressional Budget Office Study (Washington, D.C.: Government Printing Office, December 1980).

147. R. Benes et al., *Problems in Price Control: Pricing Techniques,* edited by P. Frank and M. Quint, OPA History Series, (Washington, D.C.: Government Printing Office, 1947) at 21; A. Letzler, "The General Ceiling Price Regulation—Problems of Coverage and Exclusion," 19 *Law and Contemporary Problems* (1954): 486, 492. 36 *Federal Register* 15,727 (August 17, 1971)(Nixon's 90-day freeze).

148. For a definitive and concise statement of these issues, see generally, Judge Stephen G. Breyer, "Historically Based Price Regulation" in *Regulation and Its Reform,* Harvard Law School, Kennedy School of Government Faculty Project on Regulation Discussion Paper, (Cambridge, Mass.: Harvard University Press, forthcoming), chapter 4.

149. Id.

150. James A. Mirrlees, Edgeworth Professor of Economics, Oxford University.

151. A. Letzler, "The General Ceiling Price Regulation—Problems of Coverage and Exclusion," 19 *Law and Contemporary Problems* (1954): 486.

152. Breyer, *Regulation and Its Reform, supra.*

153. *See generally,* Michael Ellman, *Soviet Planning Today,* University of Cambride Department of Applied Economics Occasional Paper 25, (Cambridge: Cambridge University Press, 1971); R. Powell, "Plan Execution and the Workability of Soviet Planning," 1 *Journal of Comparative Economics* (1977): 51.

154. R. Dickerson, "The 'Freeze' Method of Establishing Ceiling Prices,"in Benes, *Problems in Price Control: Pricing Techniques,* at 42.

155. Benes, "Formula Pricing," and A. Lifter, "Pricing by Specific Authorization," in Benes, *Problems in Price Control: Pricing Techniques* at 75–90, 91 respectively.

156. R. Olson, "Adjustments and Other Special Problems under the General Ceiling Price Regulation," 19 *Law and Contemporary Problems*

(1954): 539. S. Nelson, "OPA Price Control Standards," 19 *Law and Contemporary Problems* (1954): 554, 563. See also 16 *Federal Register* 5011 (1951) (regulation permitting pass through of certain cost increases to avoid a "replacement cost squeeze").

157. See R. Olson and S. Nelson *supra* and F. Wolf and F. Keller, "Problems of the Industry Earnings Standard," 19 *Law and Contemporary Problems* (1954): 581.

158. 6 C.F.R. 101, 37 *Federal Register* 1237 (January 27, 1972).

159. A. Lifter in Benes, *supra,* at 118.

160. J. Robinson, "OPS and the Problem of Small Business," 19 *Law and Contemporary Problems* (1954): 625, 638.

161. 36 *Federal Register* 21, 788 (November 3, 1971).

162. See generally A. Auerbach, *OPA and its Pricing Policies,* New York, 1945) at 22.

163. Id.

164. Dickenson "The 'Freeze' Method of Establishing Prices," in Benes, *supra,* at 31–32.

165. Id.

166. See, for example, Paul W. MacAvoy, "Good Riddance to Price Control," *The New York Times,* Sunday, February 15, 1981, Section 3 (Business) at 2; M. Kosters, "Controls and Inflation," *The Economic Stabilization Program in Retrospect* (Washington, D.C.: Brookings Institution, 1975) at 95.

167. D. Mills, "Some Decisions of Price Control in 1971–73," 6 *Bell Journal of Economics* (1975): 3,33.

168. See *Mora* v. *Torres,* 113 F. Supp. 309 (D.P.R. 1953) *aff'd sub nom Mora* v. *Mejias,* 206 F. 2d 337 (1st Cir. 1953) (decontrol of the price of rice would disrupt the market and entire economy of Puerto Rico).

2

The New Inflation and How Controls Can Be Made to Work

The problem with any wage-price control proposal is not that controls cannot slow inflation and even otherwise benefit the economy in the short-run. The statistics summarizing the success of Phases I and II of the Nixon controls program show that they can do so. The clear problem is that in a capitalist economy, even one with some heavily concentrated industries, price fluctuations are the signals which guide the decisions of businesses, consumers, and government. If the price of a commodity or service in short supply is not allowed to rise, allocating demand and inducing greater production of the item, damaging shortages could develop. Consequently, a wage-price controls policy can only play a short-run part in an overall program for stabilizing prices that will not induce shortages or will manage those that are unavoidable. For in the longer run, one must decontrol and allow the market to allocate goods and services. Otherwise, one must engage in democratic planning—looked upon as socialism in America no matter how limited in scope.

Existing policies are either neglecting the fundamental inflation questions or contributing to inflation. Pursuance of planned recession to check inflation is not a long-term solution. Some form of mandatory incomes policy will be necessary. The often-heard justification for ignoring a controls alternative is oversimplification: controls don't work, a conservative politician's refrain echoed by the industrial sector of the economy (where controls work particularly well).

But if we are willing to learn from past successes—and failures—in shaping an inflation program, the lessons of the past, already summarized, are very clear: mandatory controls can work and would be more effective than muddling into national poverty, if and only if they are coupled with a comprehensive program to stabilize market prices of food, housing, energy, and health (precisely the sectors "beyond" Carter's guidelines and undercut by Nixon's grain deals, mistimed monetary policy, and lack of energy policy). In other words, incomes policies work best when social conflict is lowered either by generalized prosperity, or, failing that, comprehensive policies aimed at stabilizing prices of the basic necessities. A basic necessities stabilization policy is, therefore, complementary to an incomes policy, and necessary to minimize social conflict in the absence of a growing economic pie. Its implicit aim is to make all groups more secure than they would be in its absence.

Critics of controls are, therefore, half-right. Controls would be useless if not part of a comprehensive program to deal with the fundamental economic problems. Indeed, controls without such a program would be a cynical cover-up of failure to deal with the underlying inflation issues.

For political purposes, presidents typically disclaim any interest in seeking control authority (which a president must do even if he desires controls to avoid encouraging anticipatory price increases). But controls may be proposed in the 1980s as part of a recovery program from a planned recession. For there is some evidence that controls (unaccompanied by a comprehensive program) work best during recovery from a recession.[1] Again, the notion is that increasing prosperity minimizes social conflict. However, with American rates of productivity decreasing or at best stagnating, general prosperity is not the backdrop of the new inflation. This is one more reflection of the fact that the new inflation is different from the generalized inflation of earlier times that was created by excess demand.

A strategy to stabilize prices of the basic necessities, therefore, has a dual role in a program aimed at breaking through the barrier to sustained economic growth formed by the jolt-inflation-recession pattern of the 1970s and 1980s. First, it forms a *direct* attack on the basic causes of the new inflation, which is primarily the result of price increases in these necessities. Second, an incomes policy aimed at smoothing out or riding out the effects of price jolts requires a complementary policy of necessities stabilization in order to minimize social conflict, because real growth is not present to do the minimizing. But a further aspect of the strategy must be emphasized. Because the direct, long-run reforms of government policy for the necessitites are also (and *not* coincidentally) the needed complements to an incomes policy, such reforms as they begin to come into place could have powerfully beneficial effects on consumer and producer expectations. Reversing the trend of lowered expectations is the last barrier to sustained growth. In sum, this dual role of necessities stabilization would have a third, and major, impact on expectations.

Incidentally, the "dual role" of necessities stabilization should come as no surprise to economists schooled in mathematical programming, for there the problem of imputing values to scarce resources is the dual to the problem of allocating them. Here, the social shadow-prices of the basic necessities (determined by the success of the direct necessities policy) determine the upper limits of the attainable incomes policy, and vice versa.

There is no need for a planned recession to slow inflation instead of a comprehensive controls-plus-fundamentals strategy. Indeed, the cost of recession has been estimated by the late Arthur Okun to be $200 billion of real GNP lost for each percentage point decrease in the underlying inflation rate achieved by deliberate slow-growth policies. Those who argue that once the controls lid is taken off, the country will inevitably see a reexplosion of prices (dampened if the economy itself has just been weakened by recession)—are right—unless, that is, the underlying problems that are fueling inflation are dealt with as part of the controls program.[2] In sum, there is a strong case for direct action against the current inflation: recession won't work and will only increase the suffering. Muddling-through is a prescription for hyper-inflation.

Sectoral Inflation—The Basic Necessities

This section more sharply identifies the fundamental issues arising out of past experience. Subsequent sections set forth the elements of an effective controls program, including model legislation.

Development of an effective strategy must begin with an appreciation of the special characteristics of the current inflation.[3] First, it is unprecedented in peacetime. Only during the World Wars and one year during the Korean War were there comparable rates of inflation.[4] Second, it was largely unforeseen by economic forecasters. To take just one early example, in November 1972, the Department of Agriculture predicted that retail food prices in 1973 would increase an average of 4 to 4.5 percent; the actual figure, however, was 14.5 percent.[5] Third, the inflation, beginning in 1973, has been global. The *Economist* index of world commodity prices in dollars increased 46.2 percent for all items during 1973.[6] During 1974–1975, those commodity price increases were translated into sharp increases in consumer prices throughout the world. Table 2-1 shows the rise in consumer price

Table 2-1
Rise in Consumer Price Indexes for Selected Countries

	Percentage Change			
	Average 1961–1971	*1972 over 1971*	*1973 over 1972*	*1974 over 1973*
United States	3.1	3.3	6.2	11.1
Canada	2.9	4.8	7.6	11.4
Japan	5.9	4.5	11.7	21.8
United Kingdom	4.6	7.1	16.5	16.5
France	4.3	5.9	7.3	13.9
West Germany	3.0	5.5	6.9	6.9
Italy	4.2	5.7	10.8	16.6
Australia	2.8	5.8	9.5	14.4

Source: J. Dunlop, Inflation and Economic Policies: The Political Economy of Recent U.S. Experience. 5, Oct. 19, 1974 (Unpublished Harvard Economics Seminar Memorandum).

indices for selected countries. That was the pattern of the 1970s which, as mentioned, COWPS saw continuing in the 1980s. Fourth, and most important, inflation has been *sectoral.* This last characteristic is the focus of the next part of our analysis.

Looking, for example, at the components of the CPI for 1973–1974 and 1974–1975, one can readily see that inflation in 1973–1974 was primarily concentrated in four key sectors: food, energy, housing, and health. (see table 2–2.) In 1974–1975, inflation in these necessity-sectors continued to be particularly high, but the necessity sector inflation of the 1973–1974 had by then rippled through other sectors of the economy downstream (for example, through incorporation of catch-up claims in the wage-base or incorporation of higher energy costs in the cost-base).

For the past several years, the National Center for Economic Alternatives in Washington, D.C. has been compiling the "Basic Necessities Inflation Index". The index is compiled out of a recognition that not only is inflation in food, energy, housing, and health significantly greater than inflation in other sectors, but that these necessities account for 60 to 70 percent of the spending of four out of five families; they account for 90 percent for the lowest 30 percent of family incomes. It is also clear that food, energy, housing, and health are precisely the sectors that were beyond the reach of the Nixon, Ford, and Carter programs. Furthermore, for example,

Table 2–2
Consumer Price Index Changes
(percent)

	March 1973 to March 1974	March 1974 to March 1975
All items	10.2	10.3
Contributions of major groups to CPI changes:		
Food at home	33.8	6.7
Food away from home	6.3	11.5
All energy	17.8	8.8
Household services less rent	16.5	13.9
Medical services	4.0	14.4
Rent	2.3	5.5
Apparel commodities	4.8	5.9
Durables	5.5	14.3
Nondurables	5.3	2.5
Other services	3.7	9.1
Total	100.0	100.0

Source: 121 Cong. Rec. 7547 (daily ed. May 6, 1975) (remarks of Sen. Kennedy).
Note: Figures may not add to totals because of rounding.

Nixon through his grain deals and Carter through decontrol of old oil and unprecedented tight money exacerbated inflation in these sectors.

Skyrocketing prices for the necessities of life were responsible for virtually all the increase in the rate of inflation between 1978 and 1979, according to a year-end report of the National Center. The "Basic Necessities Inflation Index" for the 1970s also documented an accelerating decade-long trend of inflation in these four sectors. See tables 2-3, 2-4, and 2-5 and figures 2-1 and 2-2.

The four measured items represent nonpostponable expenditures for most families: the rent or mortgage payment, the weekly grocery bill, gasoline to get to work, fuel and electricity to heat and light the home, and basic medical expenses. These figures dramatically confirm the sector-specific inflation that has become increasingly more pronounced throughout the past decade.

Table 2-3
Basic Necessities Price Index
(percent change)

	1978	1979
Necessities	10.8	17.6
Energy	8.0	37.4
Shelter	11.5	17.4
Food	11.8	10.2
Medical care	8.8	10.1
Nonnecessities	6.5	6.8
CPI—all items	9.0	13.3

Source: Bureau of Labor Statistics.

Table 2-4
Basic Necessities Price Index for the Four Quarters of 1979
(percent change: seasonably adjusted annual rate)

	March 1979	June 1979	September 1979	December 1979
Necessities	16.3	18.6	17.6	17.2
Energy	25.0	64.2	50.1	15.7
Shelter	14.3	15.9	17.6	22.2
Food	17.7	7.5	4.2	11.1
Medical care	9.4	7.7	9.9	13.3
Nonnecessities	7.8	5.3	6.6	7.4
CPI—all items	13.0	13.4	13.2	13.5

Source: Bureau of Labor Statistics.

Table 2–5
Rates of Inflation for Necessities and Nonnecessities, 1970–1979

	Percent Change during Calendar Year									
	1970	*1971*	*1972*	*1973*	*1974*	*1975*	*1976*	*1977*	*1978*	*1979*
Necessities	5.4	3.5	4.1	12.9	13.0	7.7	3.7	8.3	10.8	17.6
Nonnecessities	5.6	3.3	2.5	3.4	11.2	5.9	7.0	4.7	6.5	6.8

Source: Bureau of Labor Statistics.

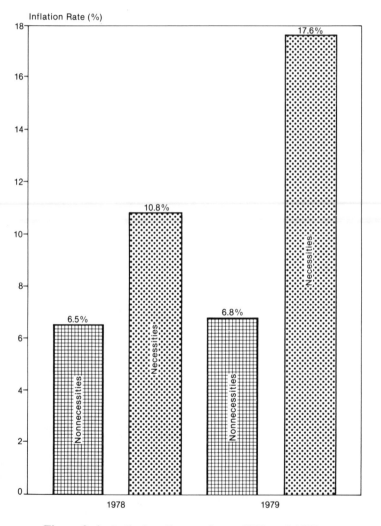

Figure 2–1. Inflation Comparison, 1978 and 1979

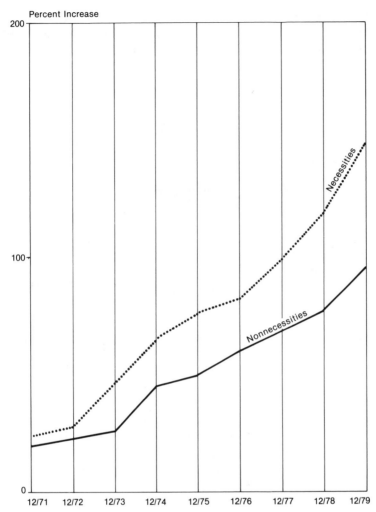

Figure 2-2. Change in Prices (in Percent) since 1967

In 1979, combined prices for these basic necessities rose 17.6 percent. Basic energy costs rose 37.4 percent in 1979, followed by a 17.4 percent rise in housing costs, a 10.2 percent rise in food costs and a 10.1 percent rise in medical costs. This was a 63 percent acceleration over the 10.8 percent percent inflation rate for these items in 1978. The inflation rate for everything else in the CPI rose 6.8 percent in 1979, virtually unchanged from 1978's nonnecessity rate of 6.5 percent. In other words, Carter's guidelines effectively checked nonnecessity inflation while necessities ("beyond the reach" of the guidelines) hyper-inflated.

The rate of inflation in the necessities rose from 3.7 percent in 1976 to 8.3 percent in 1977, to 10.8 percent in 1978, to 17.6 percent in 1979. During the same period the rate for nonnecessities stayed at or below the 6.5 percent range. For the decade as a whole, energy prices rose 199 percent; the cost of shelter rose 121 percent; medical costs rose 117 percent; and food prices 114 percent, while nonnecessities rose 74 percent.

Tightening the money supply, cutting the budget, or holding down wages or industrial prices can contribute (at great social cost) to minimizing the secondary downstream effects of inflation in the necessities, but such generalized measures cannot do anything to slow inflation in the necessities, and so they do nothing to slow inflation's primary forces.

Much current thinking has tended to view inflation in the key sectors as a temporary aberration. Wage earners are supposed to absorb the special increases and then the economy will resume its normal path. The chairman of the Federal Reserve, Paul Volker, has said this repeatedly. But as The National Center for Economic Alternatives figures show, such inflation is not only not temporary; it is the fundamental long run problem.

Barry Bosworth's February 1980 statement to the Senate Banking Committee contained a near complete summary of the problem:

> When government adopts a voluntary or mandatory wage-price program, it becomes responsible in the public's mind for all prices—even those in relatively competitive markets or that are externally determined. Thus government efforts to stabilize prices in the areas of food, energy, and housing [this writer would add health care] take on added importance. Price and wage controls cannot be applied in situations of shortages; yet no program can succeed if it ignores developments in these fundamental areas. In both 1973 and 1979, the government's anti-inflation program was severely damaged by developments in these markets for which the government had no response.[7]

Consider one early 1980s policy example. In President Carter's March 1980 budget cutting revision of his anti-inflation program (a balanced budget which he abandoned by the fall), he again had no response to necessity-inflation. His proposed balanced budget was merely political (via a proposed but never effected $20 billion budget cut in a $2.6 trillion economy). Credit controls on credit cards (a mere $50 billion out of $1.25 trillion of consumer credit) were symbolic and untargeted to the need to slow inflation in housing costs, one of the four key necessity sectors (for example, by credit control allocation of mortgages toward necessity housing and away from luxury housing). In any event, the fiscal 1980 year ended with a $59 billion deficit, the second largest in U.S. history.

Voluntary guidelines are also merely symbolic when they still leave the basic sectors beyond their reach, and are still subject to cost-of-living clause inequities of the wage side coupled with virtual noncompliance on the nonindustrial price side. A gasoline tax, proposed by Carter in March 1980, but defeated in Congress, like decontrol, exacerbates energy inflation.[8]

Meanwhile, in 1980 President Carter tripled the COWPS bureaucracy while disavowing any intention to seek or use controls. It might be said that the only difference between the COWPS guidelines program, with its bureaucracy and compliance burdens, and a mandatory controls program was that the guidelines cannot and do not work, while controls can indeed work provided that the basic necessities are not "beyond the reach" of the anti-inflation program.

Freeze and Controls Phase Authority—A Call for a Comprehensive Program

No intelligent business executive can plan for long-term investment in high productivity equipment unless confidence exists that a growing market can be counted on. And yet the nature of the jolts (from OPEC, wheat deals, and other sources) that the economy recurrently faces—and the uncertainties caused by our stop-start policy responses—force most financial advisors into a prudent retrenchment stance. Moreover, in a continually uncertain economy, we build-in supply bottlenecks which prevent future expansion. To the extent investment is limited by expectation of weak performance, future inflation is guaranteed when an upward swing is throttled by limited capacity—itself the inevitable result of stop and go expectations.

Our only real alternative is to break this pattern and to resume an upward growth plan. "Supply-side economics" is much discussed as the conservative answer to our economic woes. Usually this means across-the-board tax breaks to business in the hope that this will help increase productivity (which declined each of the last three years). But most executives make large investment decisions (productivity-enhancing decisions) because of confidence in a future market, not because of tax breaks. The General Accounting Office, assessing the impact of investment tax credits granted in 1978, in fact, found that they achieved very little change in actual investment decisions, at a budget cost of $19 billion. A supply-side economics is necessary but one that is targeted to the problem sectors of food, housing, energy, and health. Equally necessary is a restoration of confidence and certainty of expectations. The following discussion outlines a necessities strategy that could be coupled with a freeze and controls program. Later chapters detail the necessities strategy.

Six-Month Freeze

A freeze focuses on stabilizing expectations.

Arnold Weber, first director of the Nixon Economic Stabilization Program, has summarized the worth of a freeze:

As an economic policy designed to influence wage and price movements, a freeze is most significant as an effort to change expectations. By signifying the government's resolve to bring inflation under control, wage and price increases that reflect the expectation that real wages gains will decline and costs will rise may be dampened, albeit temporarily. The long-run task of achieving economic growth with wage and price stability obviously requires the application of monetary and fiscal policies and—many commentators would maintain—income policies that are more sophisticated than a wage-price freeze. For the public at large or major economic interest groups, however, these policies are arcane, and their solutary impact, if any, is revealed only after a time lag of some duration. Consequently, a freeze can be a useful instrument to achieve an immediate change in expectations.[9]

A freeze is useful to provide time to develop longer-term policies (policies aimed, as never before, at stabilizing inflation in the basic necessities) while providing an interim response to an immediate economic crisis. Moreover, a freeze period could be used to build a national consensus for the new type of incomes policy that is needed. Since a freeze cannot be sustained for a long period of time without having severe effects on resource allocation or engendering severe political strains, [10] a six-month statutory time limit would both minimize likelihood of misallocation and provide a deadline by which other measures must be undertaken.

In order to mimimize the effects of anticipatory price increases precipitated by Congressional deliberation of any statute that mandated or permitted a freeze, the statute should either mandate a six-month freeze retroactive to the date of first consideration of the legislation (or some other arbitrary date) or grant stand-by authority to the president to control prices and wages (including roll-back authority) without specifically mandating a freeze. In the latter case, some particularly large recent price increases might be rolled-back as presumptively anticipatory while most are frozen. Those companies that voluntarily prenotify COWPS of price increases could be assessed on their merits. Those that do not could be presumptively rolled back.

Presidential Report on Program to Stabilize Prices in the Necessities and Mandatory Controls

It should be patent from the preceding discussion that a freeze must be a prelude to two things: a phase of mandatory controls based on the World War II experience and the rather successful experience of Phase II of the 1971–1974 Economic Stabilization Program, but with important modifications; and a comprehensive plan to stabilize prices in the basic necessities, the true engines of the current inflation, something never before appreciated and so, never before done.

The Comprehensive Anti-Inflation Act set forth in appendix 2A establishes a mandatory retroactive six-month freeze on all prices, wages, rents, interest rates, professional fees profit margins, corporate dividends, and other transfers. The freeze authority transcends all sectors of the economy; however, the president would be given authority to exempt a sector of the economy from coverage if particular problems develop.

Meanwhile, the president is given six months to present to Congress a three-year plan to stabilize prices in the basic necessities (food, housing, energy, and health). The president's report, due six months after enactment of the Act would, unless rejected by a majority vote of Congress, spell out a detailed plan for action directly dealing with each of these sectors of the economy. It is required to have a three-year time horizon, the length of time for which the president is authorized to impose sector-by-sector mandatory controls. However, except for the requirement that the plan aim to achieve tough general objectives (summarized in following sections) the president is left free to fashion the three-year approach he thinks is best suited to stabilizing necessity prices as rapidly as possible and to maintaining stable necessity prices after the third year.

Clearly, the elements of a necessity stabilization program will be as much the subject of political calculation as economic analysis. The act does not attempt to dictate that calculus. Yet by providing for "negative affirmance" of the president's plan, the Congress is kept involved and jointly responsible for the necessities effort—adding a legitimacy that solely presidential authority cannot provide.

Moreover, the stated objectives aim to keep the president directed toward well-defined, publicly understandable goals. The danger of enacting mere stand-by authority to impose controls, without basic necessity objectives, is clear. Administrators of Phase II of the 1971–1974 controls program have stated:

> In retrospect, political considerations appear to have played a more significant role than did pure economic consideration in both the institution of the freeze and the dismantling of the wage-price controls program. Over time, the apparent success of Phase II increasingly became a source of economic embarrassment to administration officials, who had been driven to adopt direct controls and of political pressure but who opposed the approach on ideological grounds as well as from a sincere conviction that such measures are inherently counterproductive in efficient economic processes. Meetings in the latter part of 1972 between the price commissioners and administration officials to discuss modifications of Phase II regulations were little more than perfunctory review of which had been learned from the experiment and how the regulations might be made even more effective as an instrument of economic policy. From an inside perspective,

therefore, it appeared that with the presidential elections out of the way, it remained only to prepare a quiet grave for the controls apparatus....[11]

Objectives of a Presidential Report—Stabilization of Necessity Prices

The president's report must reverse the old religion. Food, housing, energy, and health cannot any longer be beyond the reach of the program, but must be its core. In the pages which follow legislation authorizing standby wage-price controls and specific proposals to stabilize these prices are set forth. For now, it suffices to say that the objectives that an anti-inflation plan must aim for include the following:

Food. The program must set forth a plan to stabilize domestic food prices in America—which is still the breadbasket of the world. America's share of grain exports more than equals Saudi Arabia's share of oil exports. The plan must stabilize domestic wheat, rice, corn, grain sorghum, barley oats, rye, and soybean prices at their target levels for each of the years $198x-8x+3$,[12] while maintaining farm income at current real levels. There are, obviously, alternative goals that could be specified, but a target price goal aims to hold domestic grain prices to cost of production plus a fair return to farmers as established by the 1977 act, subject to the caveat that real farm income be protected.

One way to achieve this objective would be by establishing a National Grain Board that would hold domestic prices to target levels while maximizing export revenue by raising the price of American grain sold abroad (except food aid sales).

Alternatively, grain stabilization by a significant increase in the present (14 percent) U.S. grain reserve might be proposed. Without an export agency, however, it would have to be sufficiently large to stabilize U.S. domestic prices in the open market despite world-wide weather or political changes. The United States might, for example, encourage (or require) foreign governments that rely on U.S. production to cover their own short falls, to contribute to U.S. reserve maintenance much as the Federal Reserve Bank requires participating banks to maintain reserve deposits. Professor Nelson, whose food-sector analysis was referred to in chapter 1, has estimated that it would be prohibitively expensive for the United States to try to stabilize world grain prices on its own through an enlarged U.S. reserve. It is at least conceivable, however, that a large reserve coupled with presidential monitoring of Soviet and other significant foreign purchasers (and possible curtailment of same) could also achieve this objective.

The plan must also maximize U.S. agriculture production during the 1980s, maximize production of beef (not to be confused with marketing of beef—given beef's long production cycle, marketing effects would be maximum over the longer run), and maximize production of other forms of processed grain such as poultry and pork, review federal food marketing orders which materially increase fruit, nut, and vegetable prices, review dairy support prices, and, as part of the controls program, control profit margins in food marketing which have been increasing significantly for the past decade.[13]

Energy. The plan should set forth a three-year plan to control the prices of basic energy as an alternative to the decontrol of domestic crude oil prices announced by President Carter on June 1, 1979 including, as part of such three-year plan, import quotas and conservation strategies. The plan should include a mandatory gasoline rationing program aimed at successively reducing crude oil imports by 7 percent per year during the three-year program.

Housing. The plan must set forth measures to slow housing-price inflation by increasing availability of mortgages for necessity housing through use of the Credit Control Act of 1969, allocating credit toward necessity housing and away from luxury or speculative housing.

Health. The plan must set forth a scheme for mandatory hospital cost-containment and a plan to stabilize health care costs as a percentage of gross national product.

These programs (raw agricultural goods price stabilization, gas rationing, mortgage credit allocation, and hospital cost-containment) may seem unusual aspects of a controls program. They are. Indeed, they should have been implemented during the past decade before the necessity-inflation of 1973-1974 rippled downstream in the late 1970s and before the process accelerated in the early 1980s. Together, necessity measures and controls are complementary alternatives to planned and recurrent recession.

Strengthening COWPS

COWPS, the watchdog of inflation, was a constitutionally weak agency, but it provides a useful model for the proposed reforms. Wage-price control authority was often referred to as giving the watchdog teeth. Unfortunately, COWPS's eyesight and hearing were so weak that if it had been given teeth—and nothing more—the only thing it was likely to bite was its own administrative tail.

The Comprehensive Anti-Inflation Act, set forth in appendix 2A, contains important amendments intended to strengthen COWPS. Many are based on the World War II price control experience:

1. Six-Month Retroactive Freeze authority as mentioned (new section 3 (b) of the COWPS Act).
2. Requirement that the president set forth his 3-year plan to control inflation in the necessities before the end of the six-month freeze (new section 3(c)).
3. Authority for COWPS to require prenotification of price and wage increases (new section 3(d)).
4. Authority to control prices or wages in any sector of the economy— authority to continue for 3 years (new section 3(e)).
5. Authority to issue regulations to carry out these purposes (new section 3(f)).
6. Authority to prohibit any person from obtaining any government contract who is violating COWPS' norms (new section 3(g)).
7. Additional hiring and funding for COWPS (new section 3(h)).
8. Authority for COWPS to disclose cost and price data obtained by the Council (new sections 4(b) and (c)).
9. Prospective rule making—procedures for protesting COWPS' prospective rules (new section 10).
10. Specialized Court Procedures in a specialized Court—the Economic Stabilization Emergency Court (new section 11).
11. Specialized COWPS Subpoena power (new section 2(h)).

These critical reforms require brief explanation. Prenotification of wage and price increases is a standard part of any stabilization program. Imposition of wage and price controls with express authority to vary the norms with respect to any given sector is somewhat novel.

The advantage of a sector-by-sector approach to control (or decontrol) is that it would target anti-inflation policy and encourage programs tailored to meet the needs of each sector, with full regard for structural, supply, or other problems both of the entire sector and within it. Under a sector by sector approach, for example, price increases that reflect excessive market power in a sector rather than competitive forces would be discouraged and rolled back if they occurred. Pay increases that might be justified by productivity gains (or contractual agreement to institute a productivity improving program) in one sector might be unjustified in another sector in the absence of such gains.

Examples: Wages and Food

Perhaps the most successful example of a sectoral approach to fighting inflation, and of the need for such a policy today, is the work of the Construction Industry Stabilization Committee during 1971–1973, under the leadership of John Dunlop.[14]

Construction is one of the economy's most important sectors. It is bigger by far in dollar volume than such key sectors as automobiles and steel. Even during the recession of 1975, construction contracts totaled about $130 billion and created employment for 3.5 million workers.[15]

But, unlike the auto and steel sectors, construction's corporate structure is dominated by tens of thousands of small employers. With such fragmentation of management, labor negotiations have been messy, both strike-prone and susceptible to wage spirals as local unions have sought to match and exceed the gains of other locals.[16]

Working closely with industry and labor, and adopting an approach tailored to specific situations, the Construction Industry Stabilization Committee was able to reduce the size of first-year wage settlements in newly negotiated construction agreements from 17 percent in 1970 to 11 percent in 1971, to 5.9 percent in 1972, and to 5.4 percent in 1973.[17] With the end of the Nixon economic controls program in April 1974 the inflation rate in the construction industry jumped back to 10 percent.

At least three different sets of variables are widely believed to serve as desiderata for unions in determining their contract wage demands: changes in the cost-of-living index (CPI), the economic situation of their enterprise (as suggested by profits and productivity), and wage rates in neighboring or strategic firms and sectors.[18] Only the first of these factors is directly related to the general economy; the other two are sector-specific. Attempts to lower wage differentials between sectors tend to be relatively uncorrelated with excess profits, or productivity increases.[19] Inflation in wages, therefore, means the creation of widespread distortions in the historical wage structure.[20] Such distortions are more the result of greater concern about higher wages than concern about the increase in or prolongation of existing unemployment that may result from a higher level of wages.[21] Most economists believe that this is the way unions behave. Unions either take no account of the unemployment effects of their wage gains or only take account of these effects when unemployment is high or when these effects are likely to be severe.

To adopt a uniform wage restraint guideline would perpetuate the inequities in wage differentials created by inflation. My research suggests that average Teamsters' wages increased 180 percent from 1970 to 1980; Ladies Garment Workers' wages increased 80 percent and all workers averaged 105 percent wage increases during the same period.

A sectoral approach to wage restraint would encourage economic policy to steer clear of the misguided tendency to fix a single wage standard on the economy. As the Labor-Management Advisory Committee to the Cost of Living Council stated in February 1973, in a unanimous statement on economic stabilization policy:

> The parties to collective bargaining agreements should address themselves both to short-term and longer run structural problems which they confront in their industries, localities and particular economic environments. Collective bargaining is pre-eminently a method of problem solving through negotiations. No single standard or wage settlement can be equally applicable at one time to all parties in an economy so large, decentralized and dynamic.[22]

As simple and appealing as a uniform wage guideline might seem, it should be opposed as we would oppose the suggestion that everyone wear a size 10 shoe. A 7 percent uniform guideline with a COLA exception is patently not uniform and not fair. It is better to focus on departures from the historic wage structure.

Food price increases are the bellwether of inflation to the American public. "Changes in prices of no other commodity generate as much public and subsequent political reaction as a ten percent rise in the price of milk, meat or eggs.[23] Food prices have historically been much more volatile than most other prices as a result of seasonal changes in agricultural production. Fluctuations in government policy in recent years have exacerbated normal food price volatility. These policy shifts include large grain purchase agreements with the Soviet Union, marked reduction in government grain reserves, devaluations of the dollar which made United States agricultural commodities cheaper in the world market, emergency actions to increase dairy product imports and restrict soybean exports, and the abrupt series of policy changes marked by Phases I through IV of the Economic Stabilization Program.[24]

Some major food processing and distribution activities are highly concentrated in a few firms.[25] This raises the question of whether prices are administered rather than competitive. William Mueller, former chief economist at the Federal Trade Commission has stated, "Empirical studies show that firms in food industries where four firms control 60 percent or more of sales enjoy considerable discretion in setting prices, with the result that they enjoy profit rates 50 percent larger than firms in industries where four firms control 40 percent or less of sales."[26] In the mid sixties, the final report of the National Commission on Food Marketing made a similar statement:

> Concentration of much of the food industry is not yet high enough to impair seriously the effectiveness of competition, and we do not suggest

divestiture of current holdings even where concentration is highest unless future conduct demonstrates the need for it. Nor do we believe that internal growth should be restrained if achieved fairly. The principal danger of impairment of competition appears to be merger and acquisition by dominant firms.

It is our conclusion that *acquisitions or mergers by the largest firms in any concentrated branch of the food industry,* which result in a significant increase in their market shares or the geographic extension of their markets, *probably will result in a substantial lessening of competition* in violation of the Clayton Act. (emphasis in original).[27]

Profits as a percentage of stockholder's equity in the food processing and marketing sectors have risen both absolutely and relative to other manufacturing sectors since the early 1960s.

But lack of adequate data constrains policy formation for the food sector. Data by industry, by firm, and by product-line within firms are needed. Such data are often not available due to the conglomerate nature of many food concerns. As mentioned above, the COWPS Act amendments of 1975 gave COWPS the power to subpoena cost, price, profit, and other information from firms on a product-line by product-line basis—provided the firms maintain that information in the ordinary course of business. Apart from the problems created by the technical wording of the amended act, COWPS had considerable difficulty developing a product-line data-base.[28]

In 1974, the FTC initiated a Line-ot-Business reporting program in an effort to provide more accurate information on industry in the United States.[29] Under the program, conglomerate multiproduct corporations must provide the FTC with detailed financial information on their activities according to particular product-lines. After obtaining the individual company product-line data, the FTC publishes statistical reports on aggregate (but not individual company) profits, costs, and other financial data for each line of business.[30] Individual company product-line data is precisely the type of information that the 1975 COWPS act amendments authorized COWPS to subpoena from the companies themselves.[31] Moreover, the original COWPS Act requires "[any] department or agency of the United States which collects, generates, or otherwise prepares or maintains data or information pertaining to the economy or any sector of the economy..., upon the request of the Chairman of the Council (to) make that data or information available to the Council."[32] The FTC, therefore, could be required to make its product-line data available to COWPS.[33]

COWPS's administrative burden would be lightened if it obtained product line reports from the FTC. Unfortunately, the FTC has met strong opposition from businesses to its request for line-of-business data. Hundreds of motions to quash requests for information have been filed with the FTC.[34] Litigation of the FTCs right to the data takes three to four years.[35]

COWPS would meet similar resistance if it tried to subpoena product-line information under its own authority.

The food sector provides a good illustration of how the lack of product-line data capability hinders policy formation. The FTC Staff Economic Report, entitled *Price and Profit Trends in Four Food Manufacturing Industries,*[36] attempted to determine, for the period of rapid food price increases following the Economic Stabilization Program, whether increased profits in four food processing industries were a contributing factor. It found that profit-push pressure was not significant in the meat, milk, bread, and beer industries.[37] But its analysis was severely hampered by the lack of product-line data.

Only 30 percent of industry sales by bread and 15 percent of sales by fluid-milk manufacturers could be studied because "most of the important producers are parts of very large, diversified corporations, for which product-by-product information was not available. Without it, the costs of producing fluid milk cannot be separated from the costs of producing any other product that the conglomerate makes."[38] Probably none of the major fluid-milk producers could be studied.[39] Large bread makers such as Continental, a subsidiary of ITT which makes Wonder Bread, also could not be studied.[40] In light of such limitations on the data-base, the report's conclusions are hardly authoritative, or even helpful.

The proposed Comprehensive Anti-Inflation Act attempts to overcome these data problems in two ways. First, COWPS is given specialized subpoena power, under which, for example, a company could be prevented from increasing its prices until it complied fully with a subpoena for cost, price, and profit data. (See section 2(h)).

Second, control authority itself, if invoked with respect to a particular sector, would permit COWPS to prohibit any price or wage increases that were not justified as within control norms.

Other problems peculiar to the food sector for which COWPS would have authority to prescribe countermandering norms include:

1. Throughout most of the country, dairy prices are regulated by either state or federal governments.[41] Dairy cooperatives maintain and raise prices in regulated and unregulated areas. The government's role here, however, is to set minimum, not maximum prices. In fiscal 1981, federal milk price support subsidies cost the U.S. taxpayer $1.4 billion despite a glut of high priced dairy products on the market. These could be suspended if justified.

2. It can be argued that 20 of the 50 odd U.S.D.A. agricultural marketing orders effectively raise price levels for a number of vegetables, fruits, and nuts.[42] Marketing orders sanction the operation of grower cooperatives in price setting. These could be modified.

3. Sugar prices are buoyed up by government quotas. A system of

market-risk sharing contracts allocates risk between sugar beet growers and processors when cane prices are abnormally high.[43] These could be regulated.

4. Meat production is subject to government import quotas and is characterized by levels of concentration higher than the competitive norm. "At the very least, the data might suggest the feasibility of controlling beef prices at the feedlot level by regulating the 2000 or so feedlots in excess of 1000 head capacity. The argument often heard, that there are too many units to regulate, is lessened somewhat by these numbers."[44]

In *AFL–CIO* v. *Kahn,* the U.S. Court of Appeals held that President Carter could withhold government contracts from companies found not to be in compliance with the voluntary wage-price guidelines,[45] despite the fact that the COWPS Act does not expressly empower the president to do that. That decision has been rightly criticized as judicial legislation in the disguise of legislative interpretation.[46] The court was apparently sympathetic to President Carter's effort to slow inflation without compulsory weapons. The proposed act expressly grants the president such authority.

As noted above, the COWPS Act expressly prohibits the Council from disclosing product-line cost, price, and profit information that it obtains by subpoena. The difficulty of obtaining such information in the first place has already been discussed. Once obtained, however, there are strong arguments for granting COWPS the authority to publicize that information when it will have a procompetitive or anti-inflationary effect. In testimony before the Senate Banking Committee regarding the Proxmire-Stevenson drafts, the COWPS staff noted:

> Senator Proxmire in his remarks on introducing S.409 stated that the ability to make a large part of the information public will result in a more informed citizen debate and give the President a freer hand in presenting his case to the American people if he feels a wage or price increase is not justified. In addition, he stated that the availability of cost, price, and profit information also should help to keep prices down by attracting new entrants into an industry showing high profits. This would mean greater competition, increased supply, and lower price to the consumer.[47]

Presumably, business might resist disclosure for a variety of reasons ranging from a gut sense of privacy to more rational concerns about competitors and the responses of other governmental agencies. A closer look indicates, however, that these reasons are undeserving of protection; concern that other government agencies, such as the FTC and Antitrust Division of the Justice Department, may take enforcement action against the business if they have COWPS's product-by-product information[48] should not prevent disclosure if indeed the underlying behavior is unlawful. Antitrust law aims to foster competition not to protect individual competitors.

More persuasive is the concern that nonuniform disclosure is discriminatory. Differences in the timing, amount, and quality of disclosure among firms could lead to a competitive advantage to the firm which discloses less information later than its competitors. Competitors which comply fully and promptly will reveal information without receiving the same in return from noncompliant firms. Although there is a problem, it is inherent in every type of government enforcement. It is a more appropriate argument for evenhanded enforcement and for COWPS refusal to publish individual firm data until there has been industry-wide reporting than it is for not going ahead with a disclosure-enforcement program.

Finally, firms may be worried that disclosure of product-line information will reveal to the most efficient firms the identity and cost-price information of the least efficient. The assumption that disclosure would be resisted strongly by business implies a very conservative underlying business attitude in the absence of information or an efficiency distribution of firms that is marked by a minority of very efficient firms and a larger number of less efficient ones. In the former case, firms which don't know their position in the efficiency distribution of firms producing their product(s) believe that the threat to their market shares from disclosure outweighs the opportunity to expand market shares at the expense of less efficient firms. In the latter case, a strong majority of firms assume they would be revealed to be less efficient than a minority; the majority, who may already have a qualitative feel that they are less efficient, fear price cutting by the efficient few. That could lead to price cutting by the more efficient firms, driving out less efficient firms and increasing industrial concentration. Such concern is only deserving of protection to the extent that it relates to predatory pricing, since efficiency related price cutting is pro-competitive and, therefore, lawful.[49] Predation is price cutting below the firm's average cost level. It is unlawful.[50] The policy behind the prohibition of predation is that price cutting by more efficient firms benefits consumers unless less efficient firms are given insufficient time to respond to competitive pressure and are unnecessarily driven from the market, increasing market concentration.[51] Non-predatory price cutting forces efficient firms to increase efficiency or lose market share. Drastic price cutting below a predator's average variable cost is unlawful because even if the target firm is less efficient than the predator, pricing below the average variable cost of the most efficient producer will not generate enough revenue for the target firm to increase efficiency through increased investment, research, and development in other means. Predation, therefore, puts unreasonable pressure on the target firm and could lead to exit from production when less drastic price pressure might have stimulated efficiency measures in the target firm and allowed that firm time to adjust and to remain in the market.

Disclosure should not be made where it would entail revealing a trade secret or would thwart antitrust policy. For example, there are highly concentrated industries for which disclosure of cost information of each firm would encourage, aid, and abet tacit price fixing agreements among firms.[52] That would lead to higher prices than would probably otherwise occur.

In sum, granting COWPS or another watchdog agency the authority to make public disclosure of individual firms' cost, price, profit, and other related information on a product-line basis would strengthen an anti-inflation program four ways:

1. it would result in a more informed public debate;
2. the president would be better able to demonstrate lack of justification for price increases to the Congress and public;
3. availability of cost, price, and profit information would help keep prices down by attracting new entrants into an industry that yields high profits;
4. price cutting by more efficient firms would mean greater competition, increased supply, and lower prices to consumer.

Enforcement

Enforcement policy is a much overlooked aspect of stabilization. To begin with, a major difference between an anti-inflation agency and any other agency of U.S. government must be the anti-inflation agency's ability to make rules prospectively, subject to industry comment and possible subsequent revision. This reverses the norm of the Administrative Procedure Act under which agency rule-making proceeds first by proposal, followed by industry comment, possible amendment and, only after all of the foregoing, effectiveness.[53] Such a procedure is antithetical to checking inflation, for it would prompt anticipatory price increases and other avoidance. COWPS would have to play constant catch-up.

COWPS is taken out of the regime of the Administration Procedure Act by the proposed amendments. Review and enforcement of regulations and orders of COWPS would be centralized in one special court, just as was done during the Emergency Price Control Program during World War II.[54] The Court, to be known as the Emergency Economic Stabilization Court, would consist of three Federal District or Circuit Judges and would have the powers of a district court with respect to the jurisdiction conferred on it by the Act, except that it would not have power to issue any temporary restraining order or interlocutory decree staying the effectiveness of any order, regulation, or price schedule issued under the COWPS Act. Business attempts to delay the program would be constrained somewhat. But such a procedure is necessary. Such a procedure was used during World War II. The Supreme Court held it lawful.[55]

This court would have exclusive jurisdiction to determine the validity of any regulation or order issued by COWPS including requests for product-line information and wage-price restraint orders. No other court in the United States would have jurisdiction over these matters. Procedures are expedited and challenges to COWPS subpoenas are given preference on the court's docket over all other cases except older matters of the same character. Judicial review of COWPS activities is therefore centralized and streamlined, so that government and private resources would be conserved in the anti-inflation effort.

Notes

1. Lanzillotti, M. Hamilton, and R. Roberts, *Phase II in Review: The Price Commission Experience* (1975), at 197.
2. Otto Eckstein, *The Great Recession* (New York: North Holland Publishing Company, 1978) Chapter 5.
3. J. Dunlop, "Inflation and Income Policies: The Political Economy of Recent U.S. Experience." 5, October 19, 1974 (unpublished Harvard Economics seminar memorandum).
4. *See* id. at 37. The annual rates of increase in consumer prices measured by the Bureau of Labor Statistics for selected wartime years were as follows:

1916–17: 17.6%		1941–42: 10.7%	
1917–18: 17.2%		1944–45: 8.5%	
1918–19: 15.0%		1946–47: 14.4%	
1919–20: 15.8%		1945–48: 7.7%	
		1950–51: 8.0%	

5. Id. at 2.
6. Id. at 2.
7. Barry Bosworth. Statement before the Subcommittee on Economic Stabilization of the Committee on Banking, Housing, and Urban Affairs, February 1, 1980.
8. At one time, the windfall profits tax was intended to fund energy development and conservation. But the enacted current version devoted less than 15% of tax revenues to energy, wasting 60% in personal and business tax cuts that would not have been needed in the absence of the windfall tax. Carter's March 1980 gasoline tax revenues were intended to "reduce the national debt", and again were not devoted to energy. But Congress balked.
9. A. Weber, *In Pursuit of Price Stability: The Wage-Price Freeze of 1971,* Brookings Institution, Washington, D.C. (1973) at 17.
10. Id. at 16.

11. Lanzillotti, *supra,* note 1 at 196.

12. Under the Food and Agriculture Act of 1977, "target prices" were established for these raw commodities based on their estimated cost of production in a given year. (Soybeans is a special case and a target price would have to be constructed using the 77 act's methodology).

13. *See* "Developments in Marketing Spreads for Food Products, 1978,"*National Food Review,* U.S. Department of Agriculture, Fall 1979 at 39–40; Estimates of Consumer Loss Due to Monopoly in the U.S. Food Manufacturing Industries, Parker and Connor, U.S. Department of Agriculture Memorandum, September 1978: see also *Inflation Update:* Council on Wage and Price Stability Paper, Washington, D.C. (1980).

14. *See* J. Dunlop, *supra,* note 3 at 6–22.

15. Raskin, "Hard Hats and their Focal Role," *N. Y. Times,* January 4, 1976, § 3, at 1, col. 1.

16. Id.

17. J. Dunlop, *supra,* note 3, at 22. See also Raskin, *supra,* note 15 at 9, col. 3.

18. *See* The Theory of Wage Determination: Proceedings of a conference held by the International Economic Association, J. Dunlop ed., Macmillan, London (1957). These "wage contours" or "orbits of coercive comparison" are ordinarily narrower in the United States than in other developing countries, thereby facilitating government policies of wage restraint. J. Dunlop, *supra,* note 3, at 32.

19. Bronfenbrenner and Holzman, "A Survey of Inflation Theory," *Surveys of Economic Theory,* sponsored by American Economic Association and Royal Economic Society, Macmillan, New York (1968) at 618.

20. J. Dunlop, *supra,* note 3, at 21. *See* O. Eckstein and R. Brinner, "The Inflation Process in the United States" (study prepared for the Joint Economic Committee 92d Cong. 2d Sess., 1972).

21. A. Ross, *Trade Union Wage Policy,* at 19, 75–98 Berkeley (1948); Schultze and Meyers, "Union Wage Decisions and Employment, American Economic Review 362, 362–380 (1950) (Unions may prefer to ration jobs rather than acceed to below-target wage gains.)

22. Cost of Living Council, Statement of the Labor-Management Advisory Committee, 44 (Feb. 26, 1973).

23. G. Nelson, "Food and Agricultural Policy in 1971–74, Reflections on Controls and their Impact," December 1974 (National Archives Record Group No. 432, Box 956, 197 pages), at 1.

24. G. Nelson, *supra,* note 23, at 1.

25. Id. at 113, appendix tables 24 and 25.

26. Statement presented by William F. Mueller at the Agriculture and Food Economic Conference in Chicago, Illinois, Sept. 12–13, 1973, quoted in G. Nelson, *supra,* note 23, at 114.

27. National Commission on Food Marketing, "Food From Farmer to Consumer," at 106, Washington, D.C. (1966).

28. Data not kept in the ordinary course of business, (a summary of business data understandable to someone outside the company) would be necessary to an effective program. *See:* new sections 2(g)(1) and 2(g)(3).

29. FTC Resolution Requiring Annual Line of Business Reports from Corporations, 39 Fed. Reg. 30377 (1974); Rules and Procedures for the Use of Confidential Individual Company Data Collected Under the FTC's Lines of Business Report Program, 39 Fed. Reg. 30970 (1974).

30. Note to The FTC's Annual Line of Business Reporting Program, 1975 Duke L.J. 389 (1975) (hereinafter cited as Duke Note).

31. P. L. No. 94–78, § 3 (Aug. 9, 1975).

32. P. L. No. 93–387 (Aug. 24, 1974), 88 Stat. 750, 751 § 4(a).

33. Id. But see Rules and Procedures for the Use of Confidential Individual Company Data Collected Under the FTC's Line of Business Report Program, 39 Fed. Reg. 30970 (1974) (intra-FTC regulation prohibiting individual company reports from being "inspected or otherwise used for taxation, regulation or investigation.... [FTC] persons authorized to have access to this information may not release, discuss or in any way provide access to such information to anyone not authorized to have access.") However, the COWPS Act mandate would control.

34. More than one-third of the subject companies have refused to comply even though the legality of line-of-business reporting has been upheld. *See:* "Public Policies Toward Conglomerate Firms in Food Processing," *National Food Review,* U.S. Department of Agriculture, Washington, D.C. 1979. *See also: supra,* note 23, at 392 n.17. Grounds for these motions to quash include claims that the FTC has exceeded its statutory authority by implementing the program because data collected would be unreliable, that the order was exclusively burdensome, and that the order to file reports was illegal because safeguards were not taken against disclosure of individual company data.

35. Conversations with FTC Staff, August 1975.

36. Masson & Parker, *Price and Profit Trends in Four Food Manufacturing Industries* at 13, Federal Trade Commission Memorandum, Washington, D.C. (July 1975).

37. Id. at 51.

38. Id. at 8,9.

39. Id. at 9.

40. Id. at 10.

41. *See* G. Nelson, *supra,* note 23, at 69–73.

42. R. Brown, "Regulatory Food Prices During the Economic Stabilization Program 1971-74," December 1974 (National Archives Record Group No. 432, Box 956, 76 pages) at 30.

43. Id. at 30.

44. Id. at 31.

45. No. 79-1564 (D.C. Cir. June 22, 1979) (em banc), *cert. denied,* 99 S. Ct. 3107 (1979).

46. See Note, "Using Federal Procurement To Fight Inflation AFL-CIO v. Kahn," 93 *Harvard Law Review* 793 (1980).

47. Council on Wage and Price Stability, Staff Analysis of the Proxmire-Stevenson Proposal to Increase the Powers of the Council on Wage and Price Stability, in *Hearings on S. 409.*

48. Short of full public disclosure, COWPS could be required to make such information available to other federal agencies. The same argument would apply.

49. 15 U.S.C. §§ 2, 13a (1970).

50. Id.

51. See generally Areeda and Turner, "Predatory Pricing and Related Practices under Section 2 of the Sherman Act," 88 *Harvard Law Review* 697 (1975). The predator may not be more efficient, but may merely have a cash reserve which it can tap while losing money on sales of its predatory products. In this case, it hoped to increase market share by literally forcing an equally efficient firm out of the market. The damage is that it will then raise prices to compensate for losses during the price-wait and keep price above the competitive level. Predation unrelated to efficiency advantages is therefore doubly harmful.

52. F. Scherer, *Industrial Market Structure and Economic Performance,* Rand McNally, Chicago (1971) at 158-182. Especially formula book pricing at 160.

53. *See:* SU.§.C.553.

54. Emergency Price Control Act of 1942, §§ 204(c), 56 Stat. 23.

55. *Lockerty* v. *Phillips,* 319 U.S. 182 (1943) *Yakus* v. *United States,* 321 U.S. 414 (1944); *Jones ex rel Louisiana* v. *Bowles,* 322 U.S. 707 (1944). "As was said some (53) years ago, an important phase of the history of the federal judiciary deals with the movement for the establishment of tribunals whose business was to be limited to litigation arising from a restricted field of legislative control. In certain areas of federal judicial business there has been felt a need to obtain, *first* the special competence in complex, technical and important matter that comes from narrowly focused inquiry; *second,* the speedy resolution of controversies available on a docket unencumbered by other matters; and *third,* the certainty and definition that come from nationwide uniformity of decision. Needs such as these provoked formation of the Commerce Court and the Emergency Court of Appeals (during the World War II Price Control Program)." Hart and Wechsler *The Federal Courts and the Federal System,* at 384 Foundation Press (1978) quoting from F. Frankfurter and J. Landis, *The Business of the Supreme Court,*

146-147 Macmillan, New York (1927). *See generally,* The Emergency Price Control Act of 1942, Ch. 26, tit II, 56 Stat. 29, *as amended by* The Stabilization Extension Act of June 30, 1944, Ch. 325, 58 Stat. 632.

Appendix 2A:
Comprehensive
Anti-Inflation Act

To provide authority for the President to stabilize prices, wages, interest rates, professional fees, corporate dividends and profit margins.

TITLE

Section 1. This Act may be cited as the "Economic Stabilization Act of 19____".

Sec. 2. This Act contains three major elements: "Title I: Six Month Freeze Authority, Presidential Report and Amendments to the Council on Wage and Price Stability Act.

Sec. 3. *Legislative finding on effect on interstate and foreign commerce and on the national welfare.*
    The current high rate of inflation is among the most serious threats to this nation's economic order and democratic system since World War II. It has caused, and, if not checked, will continue to cause serious dislocations and imbalances in the flow of economic activity. Inflation's distributive effects are neither systematic nor just. As a whole, it has distributed income away from fixed income groups, including those whose returns on savings is fixed, and from workers and businesses whose economic power is weak toward those whose power is greater, and given the progressive rate of the federal income tax, toward the federal government. Other unforseeable effects also contribute to an inflationary psychology, based upon a decade of severe inflation in the 1970's concentrated in energy, food, housing and health costs. Inflation erodes the confidence of those who put their trust in the traditional order, hampers the effectiveness of fiscal, monetary and other government policies and could, if not checked, poison the morale of this great nation. A national emergency exists.
    Since the time of Diocletian (A.D. 245–313), authorities have tended to respond to rising prices by prohibiting them. Something more is needed if more than short-term success followed by a price explosion upon removal of price control authority is to be achieved. Accordingly, a six month freeze is declared on all prices, wages, interest rates, corporate dividends, and profit margins accompanied by a requirement that the President report to the Congress in joint session at the end of six months a three-year comprehensive plan to control prices and wages and particularly to stabilize prices of the basic necessities—food, energy, housing and health. For it is the finding of Congress that inflation in the basic necessities was a primary if not *the* primary cause of inflation in the 1970s and remains the primary cause of inflation today. Success of this Act depends upon not only efficient administration of controls but also upon vigorous and imaginative attention to the "supply side" of inflation in the necessities.

Sec. 4. Six Month Freeze Authority, Presidential Report and Amendments to the Council on Wage and Price Stability Act.

Sec. 5. Section 2(d) of the Council on Wage and Price Stability Act is amended by adding, after the second sentence of Sections 2(d), the following sentence:

"In appointments to additional positions authorized by amendment to this Act and to vacancies in existing positions authorized by this Act, the Council shall give preference to economists and other persons with special ability and experience in one or more of the various sectors of the economy, particularly, food, energy, housing and health."

Sec. 6. Section 2(g) of the Council on Wage and Price Stability Act is amended by deleting the words "for the submission of information maintained in the ordinary course of business" from subsection 2(g)(1), by renumbering subsection 2(g)(2) as 2(g)(3), by deleting the words "only to entities whose annual gross revenues are in excess of $5,000,000" and by adding as a new subsection:

"(g)(2) hold such hearings, sit and act at such times and places, take such testimony and receive such evidence as the Council may deem advisable: when so authorized by Council, any member or agent of the Council is authorized to take by this act; and"

Sec. 7. A new subsection to Section 2 of the Council of Wage and Price Stability Act shall be added as follows:

"(h)Notwithstanding any other provision of law, the Council on Wage and Price Stability shall be entitled to expedited compliance with its subpoenas upon the terms and conditions specified therein, including (i) the condition that the person or entity subject to subpoena refrain from raising any price or otherwise making any specified change pending compliance with said subpoena, (ii) a directive that said person's or entity's price(s) be reduced by a specified percent per day, pending compliance with said subpoena, or (iii) such other conditions consistent with the purposes of this Act."

Sec. 8. Section 3(b) of the Council on Wage and Price Stability Act is deleted and the following new section is substituted:

"(b) immediately control all prices, rents, wages, salaries, professional fees, profit margins, corporate dividends or similar transfers to the extent practicable, and hold them at or below their (date of introduction of bill) level for a period of six months from the date of enactment of this Act pending submission to the Congress of the President's Three-Year Anti-Inflation Program, as specified in Subsection 3(c) herein."

Sec. 9. Section 3 of the Council on Wage and Price Stability Act is amended by adding the following new subsections:

"(c) work with the President and other departments and agencies of the Executive Branch to prepare and submit to Congress within six months, the President's Three-Year Anti-Inflation Program which shall, among other things:
(1) set forth the President's three-year plan, to control prices, rents, wages, salaries, professional fees, profit margins, corporate dividends and similar transfers and to stabilize prices of the basic necessities: energy, food, housing and health;
(2)(a) set forth a three-year plan to control the prices of basic energy as an alternative to decontrol of domestic crude oil prices announced by the

President on June 1, 1979, including as part of such plan import quotas and conversion strategies of mandatory gasoline rationing aimed to reduce crude oil imports by 7 percent per year during 198x–198y;

(3) set forth plan to stabilize food prices by adoption of measures that will stabilize domestic wheat, rice, corn, grain sorghum, barley, oats, rye and soybean prices at their "target" levels under the Food and Agriculture Act of 1977 (or in the case of soybeans a price consistent with what its "target" price would have been under the Act) while maintaining farm incomes at current real levels; minimize "set aside" acreage under the Agricultural Adjustment Act and otherwise maximize agricultural production; specify ways to increase the supply of beef, pork and chicken; and stabilize food prices beyond the three-year controls period provided in this act;

(4) set forth plan to slow housing price inflation by using the Credit Control Act of 1969 to allocate credit toward necessity housing and away from luxury housing and, by working with the Federal Reserve Board, to set forth a plan that would aim to lower the mortgage rate for necessity housing to below ( ) percent by (one year from enactment) without overstimulating the economy; set forth a plan to stimulate rehabilitation of the existing housing stock, particularly in urban areas and to expand the private and public housing supply;

(5) set forth a plan to stabilize health care costs and the percentage of gross national product expended on health care, including hospital cost containment and expansion of pre-paid health care."

"(d) promulgate, by rule, reporting requirements which direct entities to give prior written notice to the Council of all proposed price and wage increases proposed to take effect after enactment of this amendment;

"(e) promulgate prospectively by rule, for any sector or sectors of the economy mandatory norms of noninflationary price or wage increases; the authority of this subsection expires three years and six months from the date of enactment of this Act;

"(f)from time to time, issue each such regulations and orders, prospectively or otherwise as the Director may deem necessary or proper in order to carry out the purposes of this Act;

"(g) prohibit any person or entity which the Council determines is violating or has violated its directives, norms, rules, regulations or orders from obtaining any contract to provide goods or services to any agency or instrumentality of the United States government or any state or local agency or instrumentality which receives funds from the United States government."

"(h) hire such additional personnel and otherwise employ such resources as are necessary to carry out the purposes of this Act."

Sec. 10. Section 4(b) of the Council on Wage and Price Stability Act is deleted and the following new section is substituted:

"(b) Notwithstanding subsection (b)(4) of Section 552 of Title 5, United States Code (5 U.S. Code 552 (b)(4)), information obtained by the Council relating to wages, costs, productivity, prices, sales, profits, imports and exports by product line or by other such categories as the Council may prescribe, whether obtained from Federal, state, or local government agencies and departments or from sources other than these, shall be made available to the public unless the Council determines that public disclosure of trade secret information would injure competition or otherwise thwart the policies of the anti-trust laws of the United States, except that the Council may not make such a determination with respect to any information which could not be excluded from public annual reports to the Securities Exchange Commission pursuant to Section 13 of 15(d) of the Securities Exchange Act of 1934 by a business enterprise exclusively engaged in the manufacture or sale of a single product or service";

Sec. 11. Section 4(c) of the Council on Wage and Price Stability Act is amended by inserting the words "other than that provided for in subsection (b) of this Section" after the words "disclosure by the Council of information";

Sec. 12. The following new sections are added to the Council on Wage and Price Stability Act:

"Section 10. Procedure for Protesting COWPS Rulings and Orders. "(a) Within a period of sixty days after the issuance of any norm regulation or order under Section 3 of this Act any person subject to any provision of such regulation, order, or price schedule may, in accordance with regulations to be prescribed by the Director, file a protest specifically setting forth objectives to any such provision and affidavits or other written evidence in support of such objections. At any time after the expiration of such sixty days any persons subject to any provision of such regulation, order, or price schedule may file such a protest based solely on grounds arising after the expiration of such sixty days.

Statements in support of any such regulation or order may be received and incorporated in the transcript of the proceedings at such times and in accordance with such regulations as may be prescribed by the Director. Within a reasonable time after the filing of any protest under this subsection, the Director shall either grant or deny such protest in whole or in part, notice such protest for hearing, or provide an opportunity to present further evidence in connection therewith. In the event that the Director denies any such protest in whole or in part, he shall inform the protestant of the grounds upon which such decision is based, and of any economic data and other facts of which the Director has taken official notice.

"(b) In the administration of this Act the Director may take official notice of economic data and other facts, including facts found by him as a result of action taken under Section 3.

"(b) Any proceedings under this Section may be limited by the Director to the filing of affidavits, or other written evidence, and the filing of briefs.

Section 11. Economic Stabilization Emergency Court.

(a) Any person who is aggrieved by the denial or partial denial of his protest may, within thirty days after such denial, file a complaint with the Economic Stabilization Emergency Court, created pursuant to subsection (c) of this Section, specifying his objections and praying that the regulation or order protested be enjoined or set aside in whole or in part. A copy of such complaint shall forthwith be served on the Director who shall certify and file such court a transcript of such portions of the proceedings in connection with the protest as are material under the complaint. Such transcript shall include a statement setting forth, so far as practicable, the economic data and other facts of which the Director has taken official notice. Upon the filing of such complaint the court shall have exclusive jurisdiction to set aside such regulation or order, in whole or in part, to dismiss the complaint, or to remand the proceedings: Provided that the regulation or order may be modified or rescinded by the Director at any time notwithstanding the pendency of such complaint. No objection to such regulation or order, and no evidence in support of any objection thereto, shall be considered by the court, unless such objection shall have been set forth by the complainant in the protest or such evidence shall be contained in the transcript. If application is made to the court by either party for leave to introduce additional evidence which was either offered to the Director and not admitted, or which could not reasonably have been offered to the Director or included by the Director in such proceedings, and the court determines that such evidence should be admitted, the court shall order the evidence to be presented to the Director. The Director shall promptly receive the same, and such other evidence as he deems necessary or proper, and thereupon he shall certify and file with the court a transcript thereof and any modification made in the regulation or order, as a result thereof; except that on request by the Director, any such evidence shall be presented directly to the court.

"(b) No such regulation or order shall be enjoined or set aside, in whole or in part, unless the complaint established to the satisfaction of the court that the regulation or order is not in accordance with law, or is arbitrary or capricious. The effectiveness of a judgment of the court enjoining or setting aside, in whole or in part, any such regulation or order shall be postponed until the expiration of thirty days from the entry thereof, except that if a petition for a writ of certiorari is filed with the Supreme Court under subsection (d) of this Section within such thirty days, the effectiveness of such judgment shall be postponed until an order of the Supreme Court denying such petition becomes final, or until other final disposition of the case by the Supreme Court.

"(c) There is hereby created a court of the United States to be known as Economic Stabilization Emergency Court, which shall consist of three or more judges of the United States district courts and circuit courts of appeals. The Chief Justice of the United States shall designate one of such judges as chief judge of the Economic Stabilization Emergency Court, and may, from time to time, designate additional judges for such court and revoke previous designations. The chief judge may, from time to time, divide the court into divisions of three or more members, and any such division may render judgment as the judgment of the court. The court shall have the powers of a district with respect to the jurisdiction conferred on it by this Act; except that:

> "(a) the Court shall not have power to issue any temporary restraining order or interlocutory decree staying or restraining, in whole or in part, the effectiveness of any regulation, order, or action taken pursuant to Section 3, and
>
> "(b) the Court shall give preference on its docket to challenges to subpoenas issued by the Council over all other cases except older matters of the same character."

"The Court shall exercise its powers and prescribe rules governing its procedure in such manner as to expedite the determination of cases of which it has jurisdiction under this Act. The Court may fix and establish a table of costs and fees to be approved by the Supreme Court of the United States, but the costs and fees so fixed shall not exceed with respect to any item the costs and fees charged in the Supreme Court of the United States. The Court shall have a seal, hold sessions at such places as it may specify, and appoint a clerk and such other employees as it deems necessary and proper.

"(d) Within thirty days after entry of a judgment or order, interlocutory or final, by the Economic Stabilization Emergency Court, a petition for a writ of certiorari may be filed in the Supreme Court of the United States, and there upon the judgment or order shall be subject to review by the Supreme Court in the same manner as a judgment of a Circuit Court of Appeals. The Supreme Court shall advance on the docket and expedite the disposition of all causes filed therein pursuant to this subsection. The Economic Stabilization Court, and the Supreme Court upon review of judgments and orders of the Economic Stabilization Emergency Court, shall have exclusive jurisdiction to determine the validity of any regulation or order issued by the Council on Wage and Price Stability. Except as provided in this Section, no court, Federal or State shall have jurisdiction or power to consider the validity of any such regulation or order or to stay, restrain, enjoin, or set aside, in whole or in part, any provision of this Act authorizing the issuance of such regulation or order or to stay, restrain, enjoin, or set aside, in whole or in part, any provisions of this Act authorizing the issuance of such regulations or orders, or any provision of any such regulation or order, or to restrain or enjoin the enforcement of any such provision.

"Section 12. Enforcement. (a) Whenever in the judgment of the Director any person has engaged in or is about to engage in any acts or practices which constitute or will constitute a violation of any provision of this Act, he may make application to the appropriate court for an order enjoining such acts or practices, or for an order enforcing compliance with such provision and upon a showing by the Director that such person has engaged or is about to engage in any such acts or practices a permanent or temporary injunction, restraining order, or other order shall be granted without bond.

"(b) Any person who willfully violates any provision of this Act, and any person who makes any statement or entry false in any material respect in any document or report required to be kept or filed hereunder shall, upon conviction thereof, be subject to a fine of not more than $100,000, or to imprisonment for not more than four years. Whenever the Director has reason to believe that any person is liable to punishment under this subsection, he may certify the facts to the Attorney General, who may, in his discretion, cause appropriate proceedings to be brought.

"(c) The federal district courts shall have jurisdiction of criminal proceedings for violations of this Act. Such criminal proceedings may be brought in any district in which any part of any act or transaction constituting the violation occurred. No costs shall be assessed against the Director or the United States Government in any proceeding under this Act.

"(d) No person shall be held liable for damages or penalties on any grounds for or in respect of anything done or omitted to be done in good faith pursuant to any provision of this Act or any regulation or order, requirement, or agreement thereunder, notwithstanding that subsequently such provision, regulation, order, requirement, or agreement may be modified, rescinded, or determined to be invalid. In any suit or action wherein a party relies for ground of relief or defense upon this Act or any regulation, order, requirement, or agreement thereunder, the court having jurisdiction of such suit or action shall certify such fact to the Director. The Director may intervene in any such suit or action.

"(e) If any person selling a commodity violates a regulation, order, or price schedule prescribing a maximum price or maximum prices, the person who buys such commodity for use of consumption other than in the course of trade or business may bring an action either for $100.00 or for treble the amount by which the consideration exceeded the applicable maximum prices, whichever is the greater, plus reasonable attorneys' fees and costs as determined by the court. If any person selling a commodity violates a regulation, order, or price schedule prescribing a maximum price or maximum prices, and the buyer is not entitled to bring suit or action under this subsection, the Director may bring such action under this subsection on behalf of the United States. Any suit or action under this subsection may be brought in any court of competent jurisdiction, and shall be instituted within one year after delivery is completed or consideration is paid.

"Section 13. Separability. If any provision of this Act or the application of such provision to any person or circumstances shall be held invalid, the validity of the remainder of the Act and the applicability of such provision to other persons or circumstances shall not be affected thereby."

Part II:
Strategies for
Stabilizing Prices of
the Basic Necessities

As discussed in part I, necessity inflation (in food, energy, housing, and health care costs) is the driving force of the new inflation. This part presents sectoral strategies—and accompanying model legislation—for the food, energy, housing, and health sectors.

The food-sector chapter suggests the need for a national grain board and export-management program and criticizes the Weaver Bill[1] as rightly intentioned but improperly focused. Alternative model legislation is proposed. The chapter on the energy sector criticizes the Omnibus Energy Act of 1980 as doing too little to promote conservation and as choosing too rigid an approach to new technologies. Alternative model legislation is proposed, including mandatory gasoline rationing by coupon or by tax. The housing-sector chapter, the shortest of the four, suggests the importance of using existing legislation in a creative way to ease the very serious long-term effect of high interest rate policies on the housing industry. The health-sector chapter reviews hospital cost-containment alternatives as a preface to an appendix setting forth model legislation that tries to overcome the serious weaknesses that can be detected in past proposals.

As Senator Durkin cried, we can't burn recommendations. Flying coal into New Hampshire is no joke. Capitalism and freedom face their greatest challenges since the Depression and World War II. The challenge of the 1980s will be to shape a new order based on these or better models.

Note

1. H.R. 4237, 96th Congress, 2nd session.

3 Food

The United States is still the breadbasket of the world (more than the grain equivalent of Saudi Arabia), exporting nearly 60 percent of its wheat production, one-fourth of its corn, and one-third of its soybeans annually. But it is also the shock absorber of international food crises (see table 3–1).

The convulsions that occurred in agricultural markets in the early 1970s profoundly affected the way that governments, international agencies, private firms, and individuals viewed market instability and food security. Governments and multinational bodies began to look seriously at proposals for buffer stocks, commodity reserves, compensatory exchange financing, and other stabilizing schemes. Economic research on these topics mushroomed.

International negotiations held under the auspices of the United

Table 3–1
World Total Wheat and Coarse Grains Data,
July 1977–June 1978
(million metric tons)

World Production	1096.2	
United States		254.8
Western Europe		198.3
USSR		93.9
Peoples Republic of China		111.1
Others		438.1
World Exports	150.6	
United States		79.6
Others		71.0
World Imports	150.6	
Western Europe		37.6
Japan		22.0
USSR		14.4
Eastern Europe		14.1
Others		62.5
World Stocks (ending)	169.0	
United States		66.2
Others		102.8

Source: Foreign Agricultural Service, USDA.

Nations Conference on Trade and Development (UNCTAD) attempted to formulate an interlocked system of national resource stocks and internationally agreed principles for inventory acquisition and disposal. The negotiations failed in March 1979 when agreement could not be reached on total stock size, trigger prices for accumulation and disposal of stocks, and financial aid for developing countries' storage programs. Creation of a major, centralized, international grain reserve is unlikely. Unfortunately the evidence is that a centralized world reserve would be much less expensive and much more efficient than many national reserves.[1] In its absence, the United States remains the agricultural trading country most affected by world production variations. The reasons for this are two-fold: (1) the phenomenal productive (export) capacity of the United States, which is subject to relatively minimal weather-variability, and (2) the shock effect on the United States of policies of other major agricultural trading nations which insulate those nations' domestic markets from international market fluctuations coupled with the absence of comparable U.S. export-management policies.[2]

United States Department of Agriculture studies of variability of world grain production and trade have found repeatedly that the USSR is the major source of fluctuation in price and supply in the wheat markets of the world and India is the major source in rice. (See tables 3–2 and 3–3.) Variability in course grain production and trade is less dramatic and less dominated by a single nation than wheat and rice. However, variability in coarse grain export (corn, barley, oats, sorghum, rye, and mixed grains) depends heavily on fluctuations in U.S. production. Although the bulk of the world's coarse grains are produced for and consumed by livestock (which are, thus, grain processors), a significant and changeable proportion is used as human food, especially in Africa and Latin America. The exact split between human and nonhuman consumption in any one year depends mainly upon relative prices and supplies of these coarse grains, vis-a-vis wheat and livestock. A relatively small, but changeable, portion of the wheat supply is fed to livestock. This potential shifting and switching of roles in utilization means that both wheat and coarse grains are often viewed together in grain reserve-grain export policy discussions. This view is strengthened since wheat and coarse grains, together with rice, form the foundation of mankind's food supply whether consumed directly as grain or indirectly as livestock products.[3] As the only major agricultural trading country with a free market export policy, shortfalls in USSR wheat production and Indian rice production result in massive calls upon the American breadbasket to make up the difference, not only to India and the USSR but to their trading partners and, secondarily to the government reserve programs of other countries which, unlike the United States, protect their domestic consumers from high prices created by the Soviet-Indian shortfalls.

Table 3-2
World Wheat and Wheat Flour Data
July 1977-June 1978
(million metric tons)

World Production	398.3	
United States		56.7
Canada		21.7
Western Europe		49.2
USSR		94.5
India		30.0
Others		146.2
World Exports	68.1	
United States		28.5
Canada		14.5
Australia		9.8
Argentina		4.1
Western Europe		7.1
Others		4.1
World Imports	68.1	
Western Europe		6.6
Japan		5.7
Eastern Europe		5.6
USSR		5.8
Peoples Republic of China		5.8
Others		38.6
World Stocks (ending)	89.6	
United States		31.2
Others		58.4

Source: Foreign Agricultural Service, USDA.

Table 3-3
World Rice Data, July 1977-June 1978
(million metric tons)

World Production	241.3	
Peoples Republic of China		85.0
India		48.3
Indonesia		15.6
Thailand		10.4
Others		82.0
World Exports	9.6	
United States		2.3
Thailand		2.2
Others		5.1
World Imports	9.6	
Indonesia		2.0
Western Europe		0.9
Others		6.7
World Stocks (ending)	12.9	

Source: Foreign Agricultural Service, USDA.

As the United States commodity markets freely absorb all shocks of production variability around the globe, the American consumer pays. He pays directly in the higher cost of foodstuffs but also indirectly as food price increases are passed through and enter the price-wage base, broadening the inflation to all sectors of the economy. Other indirect effects include the long-term structural effects on the farm-sector as the broadened-generalized inflation steadily reduces the real value of farm receipts forcing small and medium size farms out of business.[4]

The outlook for food prices in the 1980s is bleak.[5] Livestock farmers are more vulnerable today to fluctuations in grain prices because of the increasing trend to feedlot operations (which must buy their grain in the open market) as contrasted with the dwindling minority of diversified farms that grow their own feed-grain. Feedlots now account for almost three-fourths of all cattle marketed, double the level of thirty years ago.

Jolts in grain prices, such as occurred in the mid 1970s immediately undercut feedlot profit margins. A long-run chain reaction sets in, reverberating for 8 to 10 years—the length of the cattle cycle. In the very short-run, cattle and hogs are too expensive to feed; they are liquidated and there is a glut of beef on the market. But in the longer run, fewer breeder cattle mean smaller future herds and sharp increases in beef prices. The liquidation in cattle herds, as a result of the Soviet grain-deal jolts, reduced stocks from 132 million head in 1975 to 111 million in 1979. Regeneration is expected to return the stock to 126 million by the next peak of the cycle in 1986 or 1987, well below the 1976 level. Yet, worldwide demand for grain and its processed forms is expected to soar over the next decade. Schnittker Associates, whose study is summarized below, expect world demand for feed grains to rise almost 30 percent during the 1980s and exports of corn to rise over 30 percent. As a result, a food price explosion in 1981, followed by continued rapid inflation through the decade, is widely forecast.

Food and Agricultural Policies of the European Community and Japan

In contrast to America, the European Community and Japan each have well-established food and agricultural policies which insulate producers and consumers from foreign markets. These policies obscure and distort price signals regarding the relative scarcity of goods. In those countries, because of artificial price levels, producers and consumers do not adjust their production plans or consumption in a manner consistent with the world situation. People in the United States "are forced to make disproportionate adjustments in order to equilibrate world supply and demand. These larger adjustments are typically accomplished through greater price fluctuations.[6]

European Community (EC) food and agricultural policies are, for the most part, designed to insulate EC producers and consumers from world prices while allowing freely functioning markets within the EC.[7] Target prices are selected for individual products, representing the desired level of prices received by EC producers. Intervention prices (analogous to U.S. loan rates), are set below target prices and are those prices at which EC agencies must buy all of the commodities offered to them. Actual market prices typically vary within a range bounded by the intervention and target prices. Low-priced imports (from the United States) are not allowed to enter at prices below threshold prices, which are prices at parts established at levels consistent with interior target prices. Thus EC farmers are protected from competition from more efficient U.S. farmers.

More significant for current discussion, is that when there is a world shortage of grains an export levy is imposed on all exports at a level sufficient to cover the difference between world prices (U.S. prices) and desired EC prices. The incentive to export (driving up domestic food prices) thus disappears so long as the difference between EC and world prices does not exceed the levy, and is diminished to that extent if it does. During the period of the Soviet grain deals and their aftermath, export levies were applied to rice and grains. Consequently, U.S. exporters made up the difference of EC export shortfall (the above-mentioned secondary effect of USSR production shortfall) and U.S. domestic food prices rose more than they would have in the absence of EC self-protection. U.S. food prices exploded while EC food prices remained relatively stable. Between 1969 and 1973, while U.S. wheat prices nearly tripled, EC wheat prices remained constant.[8]

Japan engages in price stabilization policies which have an impact on the United States similar to those of the EC.[9] The Japanese institutions, however, are quite different from those of the EC. The regulatory systems vary among commodities. The government supports producer prices of many products including rice, wheat, and milk—at levels exceeding those paid by domestic users. In some cases, such as milk, the price differential is paid as a deficiency payment to producers. In the case of cereals, much of the production is purchased by the government and resold at lower prices. Government selling prices of rice and wheat typically equal only three-fourths and one-third, respectively, of purchase prices.

Imports and exports of cereals are directly controlled by the government, for example, all imports of grains from the U.S. are purchased by the Japanese government. As a result, internal Japanese selling prices for wheat and rice showed little or no response to increased world scarcity in 1973 and 1974, while U.S. prices soared.

Furthermore, by acting as sole purchasing agent of U.S. farmers' grain, the Japanese government is able to deny U.S. farmers more than $400 million annual income, and capture that as Japanese government revenue by buying grain, for example at $4.68 per bushel at Japanese ports, as it did in October 1978 and reselling it to Japanese millers at $9.22 per bushel.[10] America's trade deficit with Japan was over $11 billion.

U.S. Policy

The Food and Agriculture Act of 1977, often viewed as a market stabilization program, is more properly viewed as a farm income-support program. It provides a floor for farm incomes not a stabilizing influence on farm prices. For example, the average price received by farmers for wheat in May 1979 was $1.07 higher than the price two years earlier.[11] Farm incomes are supported through two basic mechanisms: market price support and farm income support.

Market Price Support (Loan Rate)

Producers of eligible commodities (wheat, feed grains, upland cotton, soybeans, rice, and peanuts) may place any portion of their production in approved storage (farmer owned reserve) and receive a "loan" from the Government. Farmers do so when the market price drops below the loan rate. Thus, the loan-rate places a floor beneath U.S. grain (and, therefore, food) prices. At the end of the loan period (9–12 months with extensions optional) the farmer may choose to either repay the loan with interest and retain possession of the commodity (which he will do if the market price has risen above the loan rate plus interest), or forfeit the stored commodity as payment for the loan. In the latter case, the government, in times of excess grain supply, builds up a reserve for lean periods.

Farm Income Support (Target Prices)

Target prices are based on the historic cost of production and, subject to income limitations, are used as a basis for making direct income-support payments to farmers (deficiency payments) when market prices are below target. Thus a target income level is assured farmers. Unlike the loan rate, target rate deficiency payments do not put upward pressure on domestic food payments. Both loan rates and target deficiency payments are, of course, paid for by the taxpayer. The program is theoretically neutral in its impact on distribution of farm size. However, there is some evidence that smaller farms are actually favorably affected because of the upper limits on deficiency payment per farm, ($50,000 in 1980 and 1981 per farm for one or more covered commodities).[12]

The farmer-owned reserve is neither designed to stabilize U.S. domestic agricultural commodity prices nor, in any event, is it adequate to do so. The reasons for the latter are two: the size of the farmer-owned reserve (8 to 16 million tons of all grains) is inadequate as a buffer against international shocks; and U.S. production remains freely open to foreign governments and other purchasers (which themselves, as noted, have protective policies), whose purchases can quickly eliminate the reserve and bid additional commodity supplies away from American consumers. In July and August, 1972, the Soviet Union bought 20 million metric tons of wheat.

The question arises whether the 1977 act could be amended to provide for an expanded grain reserve sufficient not only to maintain the present floor beneath farm prices (and income), but also to stabilize the U.S. commodity markets against major international shocks. Such stabilization would significantly contribute to lowering inflation in the United States by reducing food price inflation, which along with energy, housing, and health costs drives the current inflation.

Unfortunately, the evidence is that the level of reserves needed, given that the major sources of instability are abroad and given the insulating policies of Japan, the EC, the communist bloc countries and others, would range from 15 to 30 percent of annual U.S. production, or 45 to 90 million tons of all grains.[13] In the words of University of Minnesota Professor Glenn Nelson, expert on international food policy issues and on food policy under the 1971–1974 Economic Stabilization Program:

> The level of reserves will in large part determine the probability of avoiding recourse to other stabilization policies such as direct controls and trade restrictions.... The present international context which focuses adjustment problems into open economies such as the United States virtually insures that some stabilization policy will be required in the food and agricultural sector. The trade-offs among the alternatives are the relevant decision variables. No conceivable level of reserves will eliminate all probability of the need for direct controls on prices and trade, just as no system of U.S. price and trade controls could eliminate any need for reserves. The critical need is to weigh the costs and benefits of each policy and to choose the appropriate mix accordingly. The United States cannot, and should not expect to, carry the full burden of stabilizing *world prices* through a system of *U.S. financed* reserves. The task is too massive, and the benefits too dispersed among the citizens of all nations. The United States must decide to what extent it will contribute to world price stability—and beyond which it will be subject to world market fluctuations and possible recourse to trade restrictions....
>
> Another major problem has been the tendency of reserve stock programs which were originally justified in large part as *price stabilization* policies to evolve into *price support schemes*....

Trade restrictions in the form of export taxes or quotas might be substituted for direct price controls as a means of limiting price rises. An Administration might find it politically difficult, however, to impose export controls outside of a general system of direct price and wage controls....

Utilization of trade policy levers as discretionary measures is fraught with difficulties because of political and administrative lags...A grain reserve policy is a means of stabilization which may be partially substituted for a system of trade controls or domestic price controls. No reserve system of practical scale will completely ward off the need for trade restrictions, but the probability of being forced to resort to restrictions can be reduced.[14] (emphasis added)

Professor Nelson's observation, in 1976, that reserve programs tended to evolve into price support schemes is certainly borne out by the 1977 Food and Agricultural Adjustment Act. As already noted, that act as passed into law was designed as a farm income-support program not a price stabilization scheme, despite earlier hope that it would serve a stabilization purpose. His observation is even more prophetic when applied not to reserve programs but to trade restrictions, which he alludes to as a necessary part of the proper policy mix (although subject to the risk of administrative and political lags).

The Weaver Bill

During the late 1970s and early 1980s there has been a bill before Congress calling for a National Grain Board.[15] The Weaver bill seeks to establish a National Grain Board as exclusive export agency for U.S. grains—not as an instrument of domestic food price stabilization but as another means of supporting farm income through unilateral increases of U.S. grain export prices. Revenues would accrue to farmers.

By its terms, nothing in the Weaver bill establishes a separate domestic price for U.S. grains. Although there is passing reference in the preamble to providing "price and supply stability in domestic markets", none of the act's provisions are addressed to domestic prices; all are addressed to maximizing export revenue. Indeed, the legislative history compiled to date is devoid of any reference to domestic pricing in relation to actions of the National Grain Board. And there is some evidence that domestic prices would be disrupted and raised as the Board enters the market to build up reserves for possible export sale. The legislative history further indicates that to the extent the quantity of grain flowing abroad is restricted it would not be released to the domestic market but held in reserve for export sales. Congressional testimony on the bill on this point is unfocused and unhelpful.[16]

The Proper U.S. Policy Mix—Stabilization Reserves and a Stabilization Export Management Program

Without meaning to disparage them, it seems fair to say that the 1977 Food and Agriculture Act reserve program and the proposed Weaver Grain Board are two forms of welfare for farmers—income-support, not anti-inflationary price stabilization.

A report prepared for The National Center for Economic Alternatives by Schnittker Associates, the highly regarded agriculture consulting firm, estimates the impact on the U.S. economy of an export marketing strategy aimed at stabilizing domestic food prices. The key conclusions of the study are that domestic food prices could be substantially stabilized and that real farm income could be maintained at equitable levels (for example, parity with non-farm income as percentage of GNP) if domestic grain prices were insulated from world supply-demand conditions and export rents resulting from major shortfalls in world grain production were captured and held in a cash reserve to supplement farm income in years in which supplies are excessive or farm income is especially low.[17] A key assumption of the study (4 percent annual inflation in the non-farm sector) seems unrealistic, but does not affect the overall argument. The size of the $18.9 billion decade-end reserve would probably be halved if an 8 percent figure were used. Still an impressive result.

Had such a policy been in effect during 1972–1978, real farm income could have been maintained at the 1972 level (or increased in parity with non-farm income); $18.9 billion in revenue for farm income support could have been accumulated in a public cash reserve; real food prices would have declined by 9.1 percent (in contrast to the 12 percent increase that actually occurred). Consumers would have thereby saved $85 billion in real food expenditures over the period. No direct government payments to maintain producer income would have been necessary. Land prices would have risen at an annual rate of 5–6 percent (in contrast to the 16 percent annual rate that actually occurred.

The key assumption of the results for 1972–1978 of the Schnittker study, is that America's position in the international grain markets is such that, like Saudi Arabia, it can unilaterally raise the price of a key commodity on the world market (or in combination with assumedly willing Canada and Australia, as OPEC). That is how the $18.9 billion cash reserve is raised, after all. For example, it assumes that instead of the actual $4.09 per bushel of U.S. wheat (domestic and export) in 1974–1975, the U.S. export management authority could have capitalized on the extreme worldwide wheat shortages that year to obtain $7.50 per bushel in sales to industrialized countries (Public Law 480 foreign aid sales excluded).[18]

Although testimony for and against the Weaver bill ignores domestic price stabilization as a goal of export management, it sharply focuses on low international grain price elasticities as the key assumption of an effective export-revenue maximizing strategy. The testimony is inconclusive on whether or not a National Grain Board could successfully raise export prices. For example, Dale E. Hathaway, Under Secretary for International Affairs and Commodity Programs, USDA, testified that, in his personal view, the United States was not a sufficiently dominant supplier to be able to unilaterally raise export prices without losing valued Western European, Japanese, and Soviet customers to competitors.[19]

However, if not relied upon as the *sole* tool of food price stabilization but as an experimental part of a total policy mix, combined with stabilization reserves and direct controls, there is every reason to proceed with authorization of a National Grain Price Stabilization Board, so-titled to distinguish it from the purely farm-support Weaver Bill National Grain Board. Obviously, any National Grain Board could attempt to serve both purposes, with the attendant risk that neither will be served to the extent that domestic grain price increases (rather than deficiency payments) are used to support farm incomes. It is from that point of view that National Grain Stabilization Board Legislation is advocated here. Furthermore, the political realities are that authorization of such a board could stimulate progress in the UNCTAD discussions toward an international grain reserve since the EC, Japan and the Soviet Union would have greater incentive to cooperate knowing that the United States could no longer be assumed to be the world's grain supply shock absorber. A potential for increasing foreign exchange revenue while partially insulating domestic grain prices from the disruption of abnormal foreign demand (itself heightened by foreign protectionist policies), can be reasonably assured by passage of such legislation.

How a Grain Stabilization Board Would Work

A National Grain Stabilization Board would have standby authority to assume exclusive control of export grain sales—either by direct purchases of grain for export from farmers, cooperatives, or grain merchants or by exclusive control of licensing authority without which grain could not be shipped abroad.

Revenue derived from export rents received by the Board during periods of strong worldwide demand would be collected by the Board to pay for meeting two objectives: assuring that real farm-incomes are maintained through deficiency payments drawn from the fund; and maintaining domestic grain prices at target levels under the 1977 Food and Agriculture Act (which are annually adjusted based on increases in the cost of production). Deficiency payments would work as they presently do under the 1977 Food and Agriculture Act. Whether the income limits of that act should be applied to payments financed out of the export rent fund seems purely a practical question. If the fund is sufficient to finance payments in excess of the 1977 act limits, then it would seem equitable that it do so on a proportionate basis. The proposed model legislation, in appendix 3A also provides for minimum set-aside acreage during initial phases of implementation of the National Grain Board and maximum U.S. production.

Maintenance of domestic grain prices at (or below) target levels requires flexible authority in the board. The board should, for example, be permitted to set aside some of the grain it purchases for export purposes in a stabilization reserve when excess global supply makes such action feasible. That grain could either be released to the domestic market at a later time or sold abroad and the export rent returned to consumers. Whatever the mechanism for returning to U.S. consumers the net benefits of the Grain Stabilization Board (that is, after deficiency payments, if necessary, to maintain real farm incomes), U.S. consumers would be better off to the extent of new proceeds returned. Moreover, reducing inflation in the CPI by 1 percent adds $25 billion to U.S. tax revenues, providing money for tax cuts or social programs (see figure 3-1).

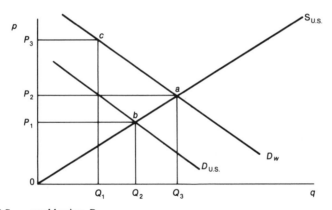

Present U.S = world price: P_2
Present U.S. demand: Q_1
Present export demand: $Q_3 - Q_1$
U.S. equilibrium in absence of exports: P_1, Q_2
Managed U.S. price: P_1
Managed U.S. demand: Q_2
Managed export price: P_3
Managed export demand: $Q_3 - Q_1$ (here equal to Q_1)
Management revenue constraint: area of P_1bQ_20 plus area of P_3cQ_10 must exceed area of P_2aQ_30, so that Grain Board can maintain farmers' real income without treasury assistance.

Figure 3-1. Simplified Graphic Comparison of Export Management with Present Situation

One return mechanism would be a lowering of the grain target price (and, consequently, domestic prices) with compensating adjustment in the deficiency-payment formula to protect farm income. Another return mechanism, first proposed in another context by Gar Alperovitz of the National Center for Economic Alternatives, would be a consumer food tax-based incomes policy (TIP)—or cash rebate—proportional to food purchases. This would have a particularly progressive impact since, with the current inflation, the poor spend an increasingly high percentage of their incomes on food. It would also have the political benefit of being very visible to consumers, and *ex hypothesi,* be at no taxpayer cost. The magnitude of the consumer food tax-based incomes policy again depends on how significant the Grain Board's export pricing power is and to what extent it is deemed politically proper to exercise it. Model food tax-based incomes policy legislation is included in an addendum to the model Grain Stabilization Board legislation that immediately follows. Food tax-based incomes policy legislation is complementary to an export agency's authority since it is an alternative to the return mechanism implicit in Grain Board authorization (namely, discretionary alteration of target prices by the Board). Model legislation appears in appendix 3A.

Food Sector Strategy Addendum—The Food TIP

Gar Alperovitz of The National Center for Economic Alternatives has suggested retail food sales as a progressive focus for a tax-based incomes policy (TIP). Carter's real wage insurance proposal was a TIP that was rightly criticized as being antilabor: companies were to be rewarded by tax credits for keeping wages below the norm.

The Alperovitz food TIP was first proposed as an alternative to other tax cut proposals, assuming the need for a tax cut to counter recession, while at the same time minimizing its inflationary impact. As such an alternative, it is an imaginative negative sales tax, and a direct economic stimulus.

This author interviewed several people in government and private industry during 1979–1980 to determine the feasibility of a food TIP, viewed as a tax-cut measure.

How Food TIP Legislation Would Work

The following model bill would amend the federal income tax code to provide for an income tax credit to owners of retail food stores equal to the value of the cash rebate they would give food purchasers. A 7 percent TIP to consumers would have halved the impact of the 1979 rate of food-price inflation and would have resulted in a 1 percent reduction in the CPI. At home food constitutes roughly 14 percent of the CPI. The impact of a food TIP would be directly registered on the CPI as a negative sales tax effect, in the same way that state and local sales taxes raise transaction prices and thereby raise the CPI.

This could break the psychology of momentum-inflation and be an effective antiinflationary part of an antirecession stimulus package. The food TIP would have a gross-tax expenditure cost of $1.25 billion per month of operation. By reducing the CPI by 1 percent, it would save $3 billion per year in government outlays. Net cost would, on these assumptions, be $1 billion per month of operation.

By releasing money to consumers directly at the end of the distribution chain, the TIP would have maximum visibility (much more visibility than the 1976 $50 rebate), immediate multiplier effect, and minimum leakage as contrasted with a Social Security Tax cut, producer TIP, or even a wage TIP.

Mechanics. The model food TIP legislation in appendix 3B uses the food stamp program as a helpful starting point. The food stamp program has a nationally uniform definition of covered foods, known to the 350,000 grocery stores that voluntarily participate nationwide. The food TIP program would have the same definition of food, and participation by stores would also be voluntary.

Participating retail food stores (or their owners) would get a TIP equal to 7 percent plus a fraction of a percent for administrative costs. Compensating price increases by retail food stores (aimed at recapturing the increase in consumer purchasing power) would be unlawful. Competition at the retail level would minimize such increases. But for safe measure, a windfall profits tax is included, as is auditing by the IRS and COWPS.

The IRS would administer the scheme, using regional reporting and auditing procedures.

Some Important Details. Seven percent is a hefty percentage of gross sales for many food retailers, so there is a provision to allow them to apply for an "anticipatory tax refund" to minimize cash flow problems, with penalties for abuse.

Voluntary participation by retail food stores could be coupled with a provision that they endeavor to obtain from their suppliers certification that the suppliers are in compliance with COWPS regulations, endeavor to obtain supplies from suppliers who certify that they are in compliance, and avoid those who cannot certify compliance.

Windfall gains to high income households are recaptured by either of two alternative options. Option A: Food TIP receipts are included within taxable income for households that itemize deductions. Option B: An equitable recapture provision (by reduction of the standard income tax personal exemption) taxes back the benefit to high income households. Either option lowers program-cost somewhat.

Finally, program length is 18 months, or shorter if the food component of the CPI drops and stays below 7 percent.

Results of Interviews. Susan Sechler, Office of the Secretary, U.S. Department of Agriculture; Robert Fersh, Assistant to the Administrator, Food and Nutrition Service (the administrator of the food stamp program) and Gerson Barnett, Vice President of Giant Foods, each gave thorough criticism of the food TIP proposal, after review with their respective colleagues. The main concern on the part of FNS was that administration of a food TIP could take up to a year for FNS to set up and could draw needed resources away from running the Food Stamp Program. On the part of Giant Foods, the primary concern was that a food TIP would only run smoothly at the checkout counter in stores using point-of-sale checkout registers (minicomputer cash registers that read universal product code and other product information from special food labels).

As to the FNS concern, it is indeed a valid one but not insurmountable especially if the benefits of a food TIP are deemed worth the cost. Long lead time suggests the need for standby planning within FNS. Giant's concern, voiced almost a year ago, is lessened as more food stores, including Giant, switch to point of sale minicomputing. Indeed, Giant is a leader in this regard and the voluntary nature of the food TIP program (albeit subject to competitive pressure) assures that where costs are prohibitive, it will not be implemented. (It should not be forgotten that the scheme provides grocery stores an administrative allowance.)

The Food Tip as a Grain Stabilization Board Return Mechanism. Finally, the food TIP has perhaps the greatest potential as an export revenue mechanism, returning to food consumers the net benefits of a National Grain Stabilization Board. Although theoretically appealing, a simple reduction in target prices subsidized by export revenues (resulting in lower grain, beef, and general food prices), would necessarily have to pass through the hands of many food middlemen before reaching the consumer. Along the way much, if not all, of the net benefit might be captured by the middlemen—leaving little or nothing in the hands of consumers. As summarized in chapter 2, industry concentration (and thus market power) in many parts of the food sector is significant. The possibility of middlemen capturing these export benefits is, therefore, real.

An export subsidized food TIP is a direct and progressive way to distribute the net benefits of grain export management to consumers, which avoids the problem of middlemen capturing the benefits. It may, therefore, be preferable to adjustment of target prices as a means of returning to consumers some of the fruits of export management.

Notes

1. Hillman, Johnson, and Gray, "Food Reserve Policies for World Food Security: A Consultant Study on Alternative Approaches", Background document for the Expert Consultation on Cereal Stock Policies Relating to World Food Security, Food and Agriculture Organization of the United Nations. Food and Agriculture Organization Publication, ESC/CSP: 75/2, Rome, February 24-28, 1975 (mimeographed).

2. Grennes, Johnson, and Thursby, "Insulating Trade Policies, Inventories, and Wheat Price Stability", 60 *American Journal of Agricultural Economics* 132-134 (February 1978).

3. Scott W. Steele, "The Grain Reserve Issue", Economic Research Service, U.S. Department of Agriculture, Foreign Demand and Competition Division, working paper, USDA July 1974.

4. During the 1970s, 600,000 farms went out of business or consolidated into larger farms. *Status of the Family Farm,* Economics, Statistics, and Cooperative Service (ESCS) U.S. Department of Agriculture, Washington, D.C., (September 1978) and "Trend Continues in U.S. to Larger, Fewer Farms", *Washington Post,* December 29, 1979.

5. See generally the lucid summary in the October 13, 1980 issue of *Business Week,* "The 1980s Grim Outlook for Food Prices", pp. 130-131.

6 Glenn L. Nelson"International Food Policy Issues", in Dunlop and Fedor, eds. *The Lessons of Wage and Price Controls—The Food Sector,* (Cambridge, Mass.: Harvard University Press, 1977)

7. Organization for Economic Cooperation and Development, *Agricultural Policy of The European Economic Community* (Paris, France: OECD, 1974).

8. Statistical Office of the European Communities, *Yearbook of Agricultural Statistics: 1974,* Brussels, October 1974, Table F4, p. 254; Organization for Economic Cooperation and Development, *Agricultural Policy of the European Economic Community* (Paris, France: OECD, 1974), Table 6, p. 24.

9. Organization for Economic Cooperation and Development, *Agricultural Policy in Japan* (Paris, France: OECD, 1974).

10. *The Possibilities For New Export—Based Food Stabilization Strategies in The 1980s,* footnote, p. 8. (1980) (draft mimeograph).

11. Statement of Dale E. Hathaway, Undersecretary for International

Affairs and Commodity Programs, U.S. Department of Agriculture, before the Subcommittees on Department Investigations, Oversight, and Research and Livestock and Grains of the U.S. House of Representatives Committee on Agriculture June 5, 1979. Mr. Hathaway, apparently, attributed all of that difference to the reserve program—although the basis for this assumption is not apparent.

12. Lin and Ingerson, *Impacts of Price Stabilization Policy on Farm Structure,* Structure and Adjustments, National Economic Analysis Division, Economics, Statistics and Cooperatives Service, USDA, August 1978; *see also: Status of the Family Farm,* A Report to Congress, September 1978, (ESCS) USDA.

13. Koo, Boggess, and Heady, "A Study of the Interaction of Weather with Alternative Environmental and Grain Reserve Policies", Center for Agricultural and Rural Development Report No. 77, Iowa State University in cooperation with Economic Research Service, U.S. Department of Agriculture, February 1978. *See also:* Eaton, Steele, Cohon and ReVelle, "The Joseph Problem: How Large a Grain Reserve?" The Johns Hopkins Department of Geography and Environmental Engineering, March 5,1976, in *Analysis of Grain Reserves—Proceedings,* Economic Research Service, U.S. Department of Agriculture, ERS Report No. 634 (August 1976) 39–55; Taylor, Saris, and Abbott "Grain Reserves, Emergency Relief and Food Aid", Overseas Development Council, Washington, D.C., 1977; Cochrane and Danin, Reserve *Stock Grain Models, The World and the United States, 1975–1985,* Technical Bulletin 305, University of Minnesota, Agricultural Experiment Station, 1976.

14. Glenn L. Nelson, "International Food Policy Issues", *The Lessons of Wage and Price Controls—The Food Sector* (Cambridge, Mass.: Harvard University Press, 1977) at 228–232. In 1980, Iowa State University economist William H. Meyers and University of Minnesota analyst Mary E. Ryan concluded that corn prices were possibly slightly higher than in 1977 because of the reserve program and wheat prices as much as 10 percent higher. "The 1980s Grim Outlook for Food Prices," *Business Week,* October 13, 1980, p.130.

15. The Weaver Bill, H.R. 4237 96th Congress, 2nd session.

16. "National Grain Board" Hearings before the Subcommittees on Department Investigation, Oversight, and Research and Livestock and Grains of the U.S. House of Representatives Committee on Agriculture, 96th Congress, 1st Session on H.R. 4237, June 5 and 6, 1979. Serial No. 96-P.

17. "Stabilizing Domestic Food Prices By Changes In Export Marketing System", Schnittker Associates study prepared for the National Center for Economic Alternatives, January 17, 1979 (mimeograph).

18. The critical underlying assumption is a relatively low world market

price elasticity for wheat of (–.25). Comparable feed grain and soybean elasticities are both assumed to be (–.40). Schnittker obtained these from "Alternative Futures for World Food in 1985; Volume 1," World GOL Model Analytical Report, Foreign Agricultural Economic Report No. 146, Economics Statistics, and Cooperative Service, USDA April 1978.

19. Weaver Bill Hearings 24–37.

Appendix 3A:
National Grain
Stabilization Board Act

Section 1. To amend the Commodity Credit Corporation Charter Act to create within the Commodity Credit Corporation a National Grain Board, to provide additional export revenue from foreign sales of American agricultural products, and to provide price and supply stability in domestic American agricultural product markets.

Section 2. The Commodity Credit Corporation Charter Act is amended by redesignating subsection 5(g) as subsection 5(h) and inserting a new subsection 5(g) to read as follows:

"(g) Notwithstanding any other provision of law—

"(1) The Commodity Credit Corporation shall have standby authority to be the seller or marketing agent for all export sales of the following agricultural commodities in raw form; wheat, rice, corn, grain sorghum, barley, oats, rye and soybeans: Provided, That nothing herein shall prevent an exporter from entering into a sale for export of such commodities at prices and terms and conditions approved by the Corporation. The Corporation is authorized to negotiate sales for export of such commodities, to barter such commodities for other goods, to accept purchase bids from foreign purchasers, and to offer selling bids in the world market.

"(2) The Corporation may acquire commodities on the domestic market to meet the objectives of this subsection and may establish reserves to meet the objectives.

"(3) When exercising authority under this subsection, the Board of Directors of the Corporation shall be designated as 'The National Grain Stabilization Board'.

"(4) The authority granted to the Corporation under this subsection is in addition to authority granted under other provisions of law.

"(5) The provisions of this subsection shall take effect six months after the date of enactment of this Act except that any contract of sale for export entered into prior to enactment of this Act shall not be affected by provisions herein; the Corporation may immediately upon enactment of this Act make such arrangements as it sees fit concerning contracts entered into between the date of enactment of this Act and six months from the date of enactment in order to assure an orderly transition to any program of export management authorized by this Act.

"(6) Revenues derived from the export sales shall be utilized in order to (a) maintain domestic U.S. prices of commodities specified in subparagraph (g)(1) of this section at or below annually adjusted "target" levels as provided in the Food and Agriculture Act of 1977 as amended and (b) provide export revenue income to farmers sufficient to maintain farm income [through direct export income and through deficiency payments financed out of National Grain Stabilization Board Revenues] at current real levels, absolutely and relative to non-farm income."

Sec. 3 *Emergency Expansion of Agriculture Production.* Notwithstanding any other provision of law, the Secretary of Agriculture is directed to take all steps necessary to maximize agricultural production under existing authority during implementing phases of this Act, not less than three years. The Secretary shall coordinate the National Grain Stabilization Board authorized by this Act to maintain domestic U.S. prices of wheat, rice, corn, grain sorghum barley, oats, rye and soybeans at or below target price levels for those commodities as provided in the Food and Agriculture Act of 1977. Any deficit or deficiency payments necessary to accomplish this objective that cannot be paid from National Grain Stabilization Board revenues shall be paid out of the federal treasury.

Appendix 3B:
Food TIP Act

A Bill

To amend the Internal Revenue Code of 1954 to provide for a tax credit for certain cash rebates granted by food retailers to consumers during periods of economic downturn and high food price inflation through an economic stimulus-anti-inflation net tax expenditure of approximately one billion dollars per month of operation.

Be it enacted by the Senate and the House of Representatives of the United States of America in Congress assembled,

Section 1. SHORT TITLE

This Act may be cited as the "Food TIP Act of 198__".

Sec. 2. NEW SECTION OF INTERNAL REVENUE CODE

Subtitle A (credits allowable of Chapter 1A, Part IV A of the Internal Revenue Code of 1954 is amended by inclusion of the following section, as section 36, entitled "SEC. 36 FOOD REBATE TAX CREDIT")

Sec. 3. "(a) DEFINITIONS

For the purposes of this section

(1) The term "food" shall mean food as defined by 7 U.S.C. §2012(b);

(2) The term "retail food store" means retail food store as defined by 7 U.S.C. § 2012 other than a tax-exempt subdivision or organization as defined in 7 U.S.C. § 2012(h) and 7 U.S.C. § 2012(i)

(3) The term "food stamp program" means the food stamp program as defined by 7 U.S.C. § 2012(k).

(4) The term "food stamp coupon" means any coupon, stamp or type of certificate as defined by 7 U.S.C. § 2012(c).

(5) The term "coupon" means any promotional certificate, discount coupon, stamp or other redeemable instrument for reduction in the price of food other than a food stamp coupon.

(6) The term "discount" means any reduction in price other than by means of a food stamp coupon.

(7) The term "chain of distribution" of a retail food store means every person selling a product or service contributing to the production and marketing of a food item sold by a retail food store."

Sec. 4. "(b) GENERAL RULE—In the case of a retail food store that is authorized or shall become authorized to accept food stamps under the food stamp program, there shall be a credit against the tax imposed by this chapter for the taxable year in an amount equal to 7.__ percent of such retail food store's section 36 amount for such taxable year for each 7 percent cash rebate from such retail food store's section 36 amount granted to any purchaser of food at the time of such sale."

Sec. 5 "(c) SECTION 36 AMOUNT—For purposes of subsection (b)—

(1) IN GENERAL—A retail food store's section 36 amount with respect to any sale of food is such store's gross receipts from the sale of food after allowance for any discounts or coupons (other than food stamp coupons and other than the cash rebates referred to in subsection (b)) and before addition of any sales or other taxes on the sale or exchange of such food."

Sec. 6 "(d)SPECIAL RULES—For purposes of this section—
(1) COMPENSATING PRICE INCREASES UNLAWFUL
In addition to other prohibitions and penalties provided by law, it shall be unlawful for any retail food store claiming a tax credit under subsection (b) hereof or any other person in the chain of distribution to said retail food store to increase the price of any food item above the level it would have been in the absence of such claim.
(2) REGULATIONS
(A) Department of Agriculture—Oversight of Administration
The Secretary of Agriculture shall issue such regulations, not inconsistent with this section, modeled on Parts 272, 273, 275 and other analogous parts of Subchapter C, Chapter II, Subtitle B, Title 7, Code of Federal Regulations as he deems necessary or appropriate for the effective and efficient administration of the Food TIP Program.
(B) Council on Wage and Price Stability Oversight
Notwithstanding subsection (d)(2)(A), the Director of the Council on Wage and Price Stability shall issue such regulations, not inconsistent with this section, as he deems necessary or appropriate for the equitable and effective application of Special Rule (d)(1) of this subsection in light of economic conditions affecting participating retail food stores, persons in such stores' chains of distribution and retail food purchasers.
(3) AUDITING
(A) Internal Revenue Service
The Internal Revenue Service shall perform its normal auditing function with respect to the tax credit provided by subsection (b) of this section.
(4) WINDFALL PROFITS TAX
In the case of a retail food store whose gross receipts for the taxable year exceed its cost of goods sold by more than 115 percent of the largest difference between its gross receipts and cost of goods sold for any of the three previous taxable years, such excess will be subject to tax at a rate of 100 percent (less credit for state and local taxes paid, if any) in lieu of any tax that would otherwise be imposed under other sections of this code.
(5) RECAPTURE OF BENEFIT OF FOOD REBATE TO HIGHER INCOME HOUSEHOLDS
Option A: In the case of an individual taxpayer who elects to itemize deductions as provided in Section 63(g) of Subtitle A, Ch. 1B, Part 1, cash rebates shall be included in gross income (Section 61 Subt. A Ch. 1B, Pt. 1).[1]
Obtion B: In the case of an individual taxpayer whose adjusted gross income for the taxable year exceeds $50,000 but is less than $75,000, the deductions for personal exemptions allowed by Section 151 of Subtitle A, Chapter 1B, Part V, shall be reduced:
(a) by $350, in the case of such a taxpayer claiming one exemption under Section 151;
(b) by $175, in the case of such a taxpayer (or two individual taxpayers filing a joint return) claiming two exemptions under Section 151.
In the case of an individual taxpayer (or two individual taxpayers filing a joint return) whose adjusted gross income for the taxable year exceeds $75,000, the deductions for personal exemptions allowed by Section 151 of Subtitle A, Chapter 1B, Part V, shall be reduced by $350.
In the case of other individual taxpayers, there shall be no reduction in such deductions for personal exemptions.

(6) ESTIMATION OF CREDIT ALLOWABLE AND APPLICATION FOR ANTICIPATORY REFUND

(A) In the case of a retail food store filing a statement of estimated tax liability, which, after allowing for the credit provided by subsection (b), determines that its estimated income tax, as defined by Section 7701(a), is less than zero (i.e., negative), such store shall be allowed to apply to the Treasury for immediate payment of an estimated fund equal to the balance estimated due it.

(B) All payments received by retail food stores based on estimated net tax credit due them under subsection (b) in excess of the actual amounts due, shall be refunded to the Treasury at or before the end of the taxable year.

(C) In addition to penalties provided by Section 6654 for underpayment of estimated tax, in the case of a retail food store which received a payment of estimated tax, in the case of a retail food store which received a payment from the Treasury under subsection (d)(6)(A) which exceeded the actual payment due it by 10 or more percent, said store shall at or before the end of its taxable year, in addition to refunding said excess, pay a surcharge to the Treasury equal to 15 percent of the amount of said excess.

(7) CERTIFICATION BY SUPPLIERS OF COMPLIANCE WITH COWPS REGULATIONS

In the case of a retail food store applying for a credit as provided by subsection (b), such store shall state as a condition for such application:

(A) that it has used its best efforts to obtain from each of its suppliers certification that said supplier is in compliance with the wage-price regulations issued by the Council on Wage and Price Stability, 6 C.F.R. Part 705; and

(B) that it has used its best efforts to find alternative sources of supply from persons certifying compliance with said guidelines whenever a supplier failed to provide such certification.''

Sec. 7. ''(e) CONSUMER PARTICIPATION

The Director of the Office of Consumer Affairs, shall facilitate the establishment of Food TIP Buyer Action Groups (''Food BAGs'') in areas in which participating stores are located. Such Buyer Action Groups shall endeavor to assist in the process of buyer education concerning the Food TIP and in the process of monitoring retail food stores' performance. Such Buyer Action Groups shall be voluntary, participatory and democratic in nature and shall have no powers other than those delegated by the Secretary. Minimal funding for such Buyer Action Groups, as the Director of the Office of Consumer Affairs shall deem necessary and appropriate, shall be provided out of the 7.__ percent credit received by local retail food stores under subsection (b).''

Sec. 8. ''(f) SEVERABILITY

If any provision of this section shall be declared unconstitutional or invalid, the other provisions shall remain in effect notwithstanding.''

Sec. 9. ''(g) EFFECTIVE DATE AND TERMINATION

OPTION A: FOOD TIP AS ANTI-RECESSION STIMULUS

This section shall become effective on enactment and shall terminate and become ineffective 18 months later, unless, in the interim, the seasonally adjusted consumer price index for ''food at home'' as defined by the Bureau of Labor Statistics shall increase at an annual rate of less than seven percent in two successive months in which case this section shall terminate and become ineffective.''

OPTION B: FOOD TIP AS NATIONAL GRAIN STABILIZATION BOARD
EXPORT REVENUE RETURN MECHANISM

This section shall become effective whenever the National Grain Stabilization
Board shall determine in its sole discretion that sufficient export proceeds exist after
satisfying the other objectives of the National Grain Stabilization Board that an
export dividend in the form of a food TIP, as provided herein, should be paid to
consumers by the means of this Act and of such export revenues and shall continue
in effect so long as is necessary for the National Grain Stabilization Board to effect
the distribution of such export proceeds to food consumers through the mechanisms
provided herein.

Note

1. A schedule of estimated negative food sales taxes received by income and
household size (similar to sales and gasoline taxes) would be set forth in the income
tax Regulation and a chart included in Form 1040.

4 Energy

In April 1979, the Carter Administration announced its intention to use its discretionary authority over oil prices to phase out price-controls between June 1, 1979, and September 30, 1981, the expiration date of presidential control authority. The Department of Energy decontrol regulations immediately decontrolled newly discovered oil (oil produced from a property which had no production in 1978). The gradual merger of the lower tier of price-controls (oil discovered before 1973) with the upper tier (oil discovered between 1972 and 1979), and the gradual phaseout of controls on oil in the upper tier (oil discovered between 1972 and 1979) led, by the end of decontrol, to U.S. crude oil prices equal to international prices.

Prior to the 1979–1980 round of OPEC price increases, the U.S. Treasury Department estimated the additional costs to consumers from decontrol of "old oil" by 1985 to be $86 billion. In light of the 1979–1980 increases, a figure exceeding $100 billion is more appropriate. The general inflation rate will have increased by more than 1 percent, according to the Congressional Budget Office, by 1982 as a result of decontrol. Americans' fuel bills will have risen by more than $600 a year assuming no further OPEC price increases—a worrisome assumption.

Carter's decontrol decision reversed the position he took as a candidate when he told the Democratic Platform Committee "There is no need to, and I oppose efforts to, deregulate the price of old oil." The 1976 Democratic Platform, entitled "The Party's Contract With The People," adopted Carter's perspective and stated that, "beyond certain levels, increasing energy prices simply produce high cost energy—without producing any additional supplies" and that

> Republican energy policy has failed because it is based on illusions; the illusion of a free market in energy that does not exist, the illusion that ever increasing energy prices will not harm the economy.[1]

Within days of taking office, Ronald Reagan took steps to accelerate decontrol, and decontrolled all oil by April 1981, six months earlier than required.

It was argued that decontrol will stimulate additional production of oil. But the amount of that additional production, if any, is small in relation to total production. The Carter Administration, for example, claimed that its decontrol plan would elicit about 200,000 additional barrels a day in 1980 and about 400,000 barrels a day in 1981. At last check, there was little evidence that anything like this incremental production occurred.

Furthermore, the United States economy uses 10,000 gallons of petroleum each second. (The rest of the world uses approximately another 20,000 gallons each second.)[2] These extra decontrol barrels, even if they had been forthcoming, would provide less than half a minute's requirements every twenty-four hours. In contrast, strict enforcement of the 55 mile-per-hour speed limit would save 250,000 barrels per day and would not have cost anything near the billions that decontrol cost.[3]

This chapter will not repeat the findings of authoritative reports such as the Harvard Business School report, *Energy Future,* and others, or the political analysis of writers such as Richard Barnet in *The Lean Years.* Those writings are there to be consulted, as is the historical record. Despite the enormous rise in oil prices since the Yom Kippur War, United States dependence on imported oil has dramatically increased. In 1977, 47 percent of the oil consumed in the United States was imported, up from 28 percent in 1972. (38 percent of the 1977 imports were from OPEC). Imports represent 25 percent of total U.S. energy use. The Europeans reduced their oil imports by 1.7 million barrels a day over the same period. In 1980, our payments to OPEC approached $100 billion, nearly ten times what they were only five years ago (and one-ninth the value of all New York Stock Exchange companies).

Price is simply not working speedily enough to bring about import reduction. The reasons are many, but the structural reasons are clear and significant: use of the automobile in many parts of America is necessary for work.

Gasoline Rationing

Since 1978, the Department of Energy has had a standby plan for mandatory gasoline rationing, to be implemented only in the case of a severe disruption to the U.S. oil supply (at least 20 percent shortfall of supplies).

Startup administrative costs (in 1979 dollars) are estimated to be $346 million. Operating costs (including ration coupon printing costs of $33 million per quarter) are estimated to be $415 million per quarter. The administration of the program would require an estimated 27,000 full-time equivalent personnel.[4] These costs would be paid by an administrative fee estimated to be 1.7 cents per gallon of gasoline.[5]

The most controversial feature of the Carter standby plan is that it would distribute ration coupons nation-wide according to automobile registration. Thus, a family with four cars would receive four times the number of coupons that a one car family would receive. No car, no coupons. Such a procedure is defended on the ground that need is more roughly proportional to car registration than to mere possession of a license. Licenses are said to be held by many people solely for identification purposes. Critics point out that this favors the upper income multi-car family and provides a windfall for those who own (or go out and register) an old clunker.

To this author, one striking aspect of the car registration rule is its national uniformity. America's limited experience with gasoline shortages points to the advantages of letting each state decide how to ration gas for necessity use.

Indeed, the major political football of any rationing plan is determining allocations for each state. Can each state be expected to cut back its oil consumption by the same amount, or are some states more automobile dependent than others?

One alternative gasoline rationing plan would be to rank gasoline use by SMSAs and permit the Department of Energy (DOE) to vary state allocations from a uniform cut-back-norm to take into account particular hardships. It could also provide that, initially, each state should be left to its own devices to ration necessity gasoline. DOE would be given authority to override state rationing mechanisms if incompatibilities develop.

Is it worth taking $2 billion that we would otherwise pay OPEC to set up an ambitious import reduction quota and ration gasoline for a year to achieve it? This may be the key political question of the 1980s. American oilfields are being depleted, and it is probable that they will produce 15 percent less by 1990 than the oil produced in 1980. Moreover, the Congressional Budget Office estimates that although American oil consumption will increase only slightly in the 1980s, from 18.3 million barrels a day to 19.9 million, world consumption will jump from 51 million barrels to 66 million barrels per day. That extra 15 million barrels of world demand coupled with a 15 percent decrease in U.S. domestic production will put enormous pressure on the world price of oil.

Americans are already paying $90 billion a year for imported oil. Consequently, a strengthened form of a standby rationing plan is essential if we are to avoid deep recession following a mid–1980s oil jolt.

Nearly forty years ago, an eminent economist offered a very plausible explanation of why rationing of a necessity in response to a sudden jolt is considered fair by many people:

> Public opinion tends to accept the distribution of effective demand as equitable if it leads to an egalitarian, or nearly egalitarian, distribution of all *necessities*. Inequalities of income and wealth, however great they may be, will not be considered oppressive as long as all necessities are cheap and plentiful enough to be available in sufficient quantities even to the lowest income groups. Conversely, even slight inequalities of income will be

regarded as unjust if one or more necessities are short—that is, so scarce and expensive as to become the privilege of the well-to-do.

...a shortage can be eliminated not only by increasing supplies but also by mitigating inequalities in the distribution of effective demand. The extent to which inequalities must be mitigated in order to eliminate shortages, therefore, is independent of the number of necessities that are short and depends only on the supply and demand conditions of the necessity that is the most short. The elimination of one single but severe shortage may require the complete equalization of effective demand.

Remembering that the elimination of only one single shortage may require the complete equalization of income and wealth, we immediately see that if the shortages are few and severe, it is simpler to distribute the short necessities independent of the market mechanism.[6]

More recently, economist Walter Salant has extended the Scitovsky theses by setting forth its implications for alternative price and rationing schemes.[7] Among the schemes Salant set forth, a combination of two of them seem most promising: Following a severe oil price-jolt, there could be a period of coupon-rationing where the coupons are legally negotiable (that is, a white market). This would directly permit a restriction of demand to the level of supply, and would lead to an equilibrium which would serve as the basis of the second stage. In the second stage, negotiable coupons would be replaced by an excise tax equal to the level of the rationed price of gasoline plus the value of the coupon in equilibrium in the white market. Proceeds of the excise tax could then be rebated proportionally to initial allocation of ration coupons (or in another equitable manner).

As an alternative to recession, America should consider such a standby two-step rationing plan for the late 1980s. Should oil jump from $40 to $75 per barrel in a single year, the coupons (already printed) could be issued based on car ownership (or otherwise, should a state-by-state rule be followed). As quickly as possible, however, negotiable coupons could be replaced by the second step: tax-rationing, which would be cheaper and much easier to administer. Tax-rationing would also permit a fairer allocation of the ration than car ownership, especially if government transfer recipients (such as families receiving food stamps) were eligible, as well as taxpayers, to receive their tax-ration dividend. (See appendix 4A.)

Enacting an Energy Program

Synthetic Fuels

The United States faces an unprecedented threat to its national security and to its economic and political future. Since the oil embargo of 1973–1974,

U.S. oil imports have increased more than 25 percent, from 6.3 million barrels per day to 8 million barrels per day. The transportation and chemical feedstock industries alone consumed over 10 million barrels per day in 1979; this exceeded our total 1978 domestic petroleum production of 9.8 million barrels per day. Moreover, out of 17.7 million barrels per day of petroleum used in 1978, only 3.7 million barrels per day could be displaced in the short-run by other nonliquid or gaseous fuels.

We have already had a painful experience of the economic consequences of our continued dependence on imported oil resources. We have had two oil jolt-induced recessions since 1973 and continued stagnation. Consumers of transportation fuel have experienced massive inconvenience at times and changes in consumer habits. Rationing would spread inconvenience even as it spread the impact of a jolt. Other strategies are necessary.

Even should all national energy conservation proposals be successful and conventional energy supplies be forthcoming, in 1990 the United States still would have to import approximately 6.5 to 7.5 million barrels of oil per day. Conservation alone cannot satisfy our future energy needs. The United States will need large amounts of new liquid fuel sources. Since there is no practical substitute for our present transportation system it would not be prudent to delay the development of new liquid fuel sources. Synthetic fuels have the potential for providing significant amounts of such future energy supplies but, the establishment of a synthetic fuels industry, unlike previous experiences with rubber and other critical materials, is far too large an undertaking to be implemented in a few months under emergency, embargo, or war conditions. Despite increased national attention, the commercialization of synthetic fuels such as coal gasification and liquefaction, oil shale, and biomass, in the absence of a national synthetic fuels effort will be plagued by uncertainty. Yet the obstacles to commercialization of synthetic fuels could be overcome under definitive federal policies.

Since 1943, the Senate Committee on Energy and Natural Resources and its predecessor, the Committee on Interior and Insular Affairs, have supported establishment of a National Synthetic Fuels policy. In 1944, the chairman of the committee, Senator Joseph C. O'Mahoney, wrote:

> There will be plenty of gasoline...but only if the United States rapidly expands its program for the production of synthetic fuels. Without such a program we shall become an importer of petroleum and thus dependent upon other lands and other peoples for the fuel supply we must have to maintain the commercial and industrial leadership which America now enjoys...

> Petroleum products can be made from coal, and the coal supplies in the United States are so large that we need not worry about them for the next several hundred years....[8]

Subsequently, between 1944 and 1955, a comprehensive synthetic fuel program was undertaken by the Department of the Interior under the O'Mahoney-Randolph Synthetic Liquid Fuels Act of 1944 (Public Law 78-290). Demonstration plants were constructed and operated to produce synthetic liquid fuels from coal, oil shale, agricultural and forestry products, and other substances in order to conserve and increase the oil resources of the United States. Over an 11 year period from 1944 to 1955, when the program was terminated, approximately $82 million was expended for research on synthetic fuels.

Following termination of that program, the Senate's National Fuels and Energy study group (S. Res. 105, 87th Congress) on September 21, 1962, identified "the role of government-sponsored research in the fuels and energy industries" as one of 12 major policy issues requiring resolution by the Congress.

In the early 1970s the Senate's interest in synthetic liquid and gaseous fuels was revitalized as the United States became an energy importer and the price of foreign oil began to rise dramatically.

In 1972, Senator Jackson, along with 15 cosponsors, introduced S. 1846 (92nd Congress) to establish a Coal Gasification Development Corporation. The proposal was opposed by the Nixon Administration and no final action was taken.

In the 93rd Congress, Senator Jackson and 27 cosponsors introduced the National Energy Research and Development Policy Act of 1973. The bill as reported established a comprehensive national energy research and development program with the objective of establishing "within 10 years the option and the capability for the United States to become energy self-sufficient" (Senate Report No. 93-589). Specifically addressed in the bill was the establishment of joint federal-industrial corporations to foster commercial-scale demonstration of coal gasification, oil shale, and coal liquefaction, as well as advanced power cycle and geothermal energy.

This measure, later enacted as the Federal Non-Nuclear Energy Research and Development Act of 1974 (Public Law 93-577) authorizes the Department of Energy (then the Energy Research and Development Administration) to undertake a wide range of joint government and industry energy research and development activities. The statute authorizes the department to guarantee product prices or make purchase agreements as well as to establish federal corporations or contract for government-owned and contractor-operated energy facilities.

Subsequently, in his 1975 State of the Union Message, President Ford recognized the need for a national synthetic fuels program. The Chief Executive proposed a national synthetic fuels commercialization program capable by 1985 of producing the equivalent of one million barrels of oil per day.

Almost simultaneously two reports were released by the Executive Branch. The first, the June 28, 1975 Energy Research Plan of the Energy Research and Development Administration (ERDA), envisioned 140 synthetic oil and natural gas plants by the year 2000, each capable of producing the equivalent of 50,000 barrels of oil per day from coal.

The second, a report of an interagency task force created by President Ford, in July, 1975, discussed three 1985 national synthetic fuel production goals: 350,000 barrels per day, 1 million barrels per day, or 1.7 million barrels per day.

The task force recommendation was that the 350,000 barrel per day program be installed immediately, but in a way which did not preclude achieving the 1 million barrel per day goal by 1985. It was suggested that by deferring until later in the 10-year period the decision to commit firmly to that goal, additional information would be available for further expansion of the program, thus maximizing the benefits and reducing the economic and environmental costs.

In October, 1975, the Ford Administration under the leadership of Vice President Rockefeller, as Chairman of the Domestic Council, proposed a $100 billion Energy Independency Authority (EIA), a government corporation with authority to provide financial assistance for those sectors of the economy important to the attainment of energy independence for the United States. The main purpose of the EIA would have been to encourage the development of domestic energy sources or the conservation of energy, and to hasten the commercial operation of new technologies, with a goal of energy independence by 1985. To the extent practicable, the financial assistance was to be as loans or loan guarantees to private business concerns. However, the EIA was to be permitted to invest directly in energy-related enterprises and to guarantee prices.

The Senate repeatedly considered proposals aimed to achieve a national synthetic fuels capability. In 1975, the Senate approved the Synthetic Fuels Act which authorized $5 billion in loan guarantees to foster new nonnuclear energy technologies. The Committee report stated:

Greater Federal incentives are needed to cut the Gordian Knot of economics for the first generation of pioneer synthetic fuel plants in this country. The marketplace does not now provide sufficient incentives or an adequate mechanism for encouragement of the establishment of this industry.[9]

However, the House of Representatives disapproved the Senate loan guarantee provision.

In 1977, the Senate approved for the third time an amendment to the fiscal year 1978 ERDA authorization bill to provide a case-by-case procedure for authorizing loan guarantees for indivudual synthetic fuel projects. The Senate amendment was incorporated into the ERDA fiscal year 1978 authorization bill and it was subsequently enacted into law, Public Law 95–238.

In summary, with enactment of Public Law 95–238, the Department of Energy was provided loan guarantee authority to complement the earlier-enacted powers to undertake loans, price guarantees, and purchase agreements as well as authority to undertake government-owned contractor-operated synthetic fuel projects.

The history of federal policy toward synthetic fuels just related displays nearly 40 years of congressional recognition of the potential for supplementing petroleum-based fuels with synthetics created from plentiful domestic energy resources. At every step in the policy process, there has been general agreement on the need for actual operating experience for several commercial-sized demonstration plants. In many instances there has been strong support for an agressive effort to achieve substantial production of fuels from synthetic sources. But overall consensus on a set of proposals is built very slowly.

In recent years, as the prospect of continued national strategic and economic vulnerability to imported petroleum has become evident, Republican and Democratic administrations have both recommended programs of substantial federal financial assistance to establish a synthetic fuel capability based upon coal, oil shale, biomass, and plentiful and secure domestic energy sources.

The Congress, similarly, has supported research and development of the relevant synthetics fuels technologies and has already authorized financial support for demonstration plants.

Despite this evidence of support, no large-scale demonstrations of any such techology have yet been undertaken. Indeed, the United States has lagged behind many nations with less economic ability, fewer resources, and perhaps less urgent need for such new energy sources.

One of the first major uses of coal liquefaction was in Germany where, during World War II, large-scale operations produced up to 90 percent of the peak war-time aviation and motor fuel supply. Much of the German production of oil, over 5 million tons per year, was obtained from some 25 liquefaction plants.

In 1955, the Republic of South Africa began operation of a coal liquefaction plant called SASOL I, which is still in operation. This facility is a state-owned petrochemical and fuel complex which converts coal into oil, gas, and petrochemicals. The plant uses as part of its operation a gas synthesis process known as the Fisher-Tropsch process to produce liquid fuels and petrochemicals from gaseous mixtures of carbon monoxide and hydrogen gas by using steam and oxygen to gasify coal. With the use of this technology and other advanced processes, the SASOL I complex is capable of producing several thousand barrels of oil per day and an array of petrochemical products.

Canada is developiong its tar sands; South Africa is greatly expanding its existing coal liquefaction capability; and China annually produces a portion of its oil from shale. The Republic of South Africa's government publicly announced that a third liquefaction plant, SASOL III, had been authorized and is expected to be operational before 1985. Estimates of the capital cost of this plant vary from $3.8 to $5.7 billion. The three SASOL plants are expected to give this African country, which is now 90 percent dependent on imported petroleum, the capacity to provide 50 percent of its needs for liquid fuels. That national effort is reminiscent of our space goals and accomplishments of the 1960s.

Domestically, we are still immersed in arguments over the potential merits, hazards, and economic viability of synthetic fuels as part of our energy future.

Our present policy choices would be based upon solid experience rather than speculation if a few demonstrations had been initiated as proposed in 1971, or even if the authorities actually enacted by the Congress in 1974 had been implemented. In each instance, however, suggestions that delay would improve the technological basis for such undertakings, reluctance to make the financial commitments necessary, and the idle hope that industry would enter into such ventures on its own have sapped the will to proceed. The initial decisions to embark upon the inevitable vital exploration of a major option in energy policy have been consistently stifled in the annual budgetary process and the vagaries of bureaucratic decisionmaking.

In January, 1976, the Congressional Budget Office characterized the circumstances under which a federal synthetic fuel program could be justified:

> A synthetic fuels commercialization program can be justified if the production of some amount of synthetic fuel in an appropriate time frame is itself considered worthwhile. The two relevant time frames are 1975 and 1985 and beyond 1985. Production of synthetic fuels would be worthwhile if their costs (at some point, presumably beyond 1985) were lower than the costs of equivalent quantities of energy provided through alternatives...where the costs...reflect the possibility of embargo or further price increases.[10]

These circumstances now exist in the United States. But a September 7, 1979, report of the Congressional Budget Office pointed out:

> The private sector has not as yet been willing to invest the approximately $2 billion necessary to build a synfuel plant large enough to take advantage of the economies of scale common to such processes. This is because they feel that the various risks involved are too high. Not only are there techno-

logical, cost, and regulatory risks, but there is also uncertainty about the future level of prices set by the Oil Producing and Exporting Countries (OPEC).

In developing a synfuels program, the Congress should consider choosing a financing mechanism—whether it be loans, loan guarantees, or price guarantees—under which the government would absorb the risk that future OPEC prices will not be as high as currently anticipated. Since the nation as a whole benefits from lower OPEC prices, the government could absorb that risk. On the other hand, the technological and cost risks could be absorbed by the private sector, which traditionally accepts these risks in making investment decisions. Such a separation of risks would provide the private sector with sufficient incentive to construct and operate synthetic fuel plants efficiently.[11]

Near-Term Synthetic Fuel Technologies. Whether or not the United States could construct sufficient numbers of synthetic fuel plants to achieve a goal of 1.5 million barrels per day by 1990 is very uncertain.

In 1979, the Senate Committee on Energy and Natural Resources published a report prepared by the Congressional Research Service entitled, "Synthetic Fuels From Coal: Status and Outlook of Coal Gasification and Liquefaction." Examples of the types of coal gasification and liquefaction processes that might receive Federal support are as follows.

Coal Gasification. Coal gasification is a chemical technology in which pulverized coal is converted into combustible gas which may be of low-, medium-, or high-Btu (heat) content. In its simplest form, the gasification of coal requires, first, the heating of the coal and then the reaction of its carbon and hydrogen content with steam to produce carbon monoxide, carbon dioxide, hydrogen, and methane. In general, gasification reactions are based on thermal decomposition (that is, the application of heat to break down the structure) of coal, and gasification or combustion of the resulting char. As is the case with conventional coal burning boilers, huge quantities of coal ash must be disposed of.

Coal gasification processes have been used for over a hundred years. During the nineteenth and twentieth centuries, gas from coal was produced in the United States and Europe to serve a variety of needs, such as lighting, cooking, and industrial purposes. Nearly every major city in the eastern United States once had a coal-gas plant and accompanying cylindrical storage tanks that stood near them. By the middle 1920s an estimated 11,000 coal gas producers were used in the United States: 6,500 in steel plants, 1,500 in glass plants, 1,500 in ceramics and lime-burning plants, 1,000 in gas utilities, and 500 in metallurgical and chemical plants.

Although the greatest portion of this coal (or producer) gas was made from bituminous coal, operators could have used almost any fuel from anthracite to wood wastes. The systems gradually disappeared after World War II as natural gas began to be distributed nationally by pipeline. After coal-gas lost its markets in the United States, coal gasification technologies were further advanced abroad.

The emerging U.S. coal gasification industry is developing along two major routes: low- and medium-Btu systems for use primarily in industrial and utility markets, and high-Btu systems for use primarily in the residential and industrial markets.

High-Btu Surface Coal Gasification. Several coal gasification processes are under development to produce high-Btu gas as a substitute for natural gas. Essentially all the processes employ the same chemical process. Process variations arise from the selection of, for example, fixed-bed, fluid-bed, or entrained-bed operation, pressure, temperature, and so on, the choice being determined by the coal-feed characteristics and product-quality requirements.

Second and third generation processes represent variations on first generation technologies in an effort to reduce cost, improve efficiency, or reduce environmental effects. The status of the various first general and advanced—second or third generation—high Btu gasification processes is shown in table 4–1. This table demonstrates that there are several processes which proponents claim are capable of producing oil at a price less than the current price of OPEC oil. Although these estimates are optimistic, they do allow for the time to construct a pilot plant when necessary, but this schedule does not allow for unusual delays to obtain environmental or regulatory permits.

Typically, a coal gasification plant would cost approximately $1.5 billion. However, the United States presently has over $100 billion invested in its gas transmission, distribution, and end-user equipment system. On an economic basis, keeping these gas pipelines full, even with higher-priced synthetics, and extension of the useful life of present pipeline systems, is cheaper for the American consumer than creating new systems.

Similarly, the capital required to produce and deliver a unit of energy in the form of synthetic natural gas from coal is also less than that required to produce and deliver electricity from coal.

However, the national effort required to replace 1 million barrels of oil imports per day with synthetic gaseous and liquid fuels would require approximately 25 different plants each employing about 20 gasifiers or some 500 gasification units. Each plant would cost about $1.5 billion. Thus, in order to achieve a production goal of 1 milion barrels, a capital investment of about $35 billion would be required. Construction of each plant would take about 1,800 craftsmen and journeymen, working 3 years.

Medium-Btu Coal Gasification. Over 100 medium-Btu gasification plants are operational around the world. However, none are in the United States. Several processes are commercially available.

Table 4-1
Oil-Shale Recovery Comparative Costs per Barrel and Comparative Selling Prices at 20 Percent and 15 Percent Discounted Cash Flow—Return on Investment

Process	Barrels per Day Capacity	Daily Barrels Capital	Barrels Operating Cost	Selling Price DCFROI 20 Percent	15 Percent
Tosco II[a]	50,000	$13.260	$ 4.40	$17.00	$13.00
Paraho[b]	50,000	12,000	4.30	17.00	13.00
Paraho (Paraho estimate)[c]	99,200	11,800	4.10	15.50	11.50
Occidental[d]	57,000	7,015	4.40	14.00	11.00
Combined TOSCO modified in situ[e]	82,890	8,615	3.80	15.00	12.00
Superior type	43,110	18,642[h]	14.40	19.90	15.00
Shell:					
In situ only	30,500	17,380	5.39	22.50[i]	18.00[i]
Surface only					
TOSCO	52,300	17,690	2.70	25.00[i]	19.25[i]
Combination	54,100	15,500	3.49	21.00[i]	16.00[i]

Source: Laramie Energy Research Center.
[a]"Shale Oil Economics," John A. Whitcombs, TOSCO Corp., January 1977.
[b]An Economic Evaluation Using Thirty GPT Shale and Producing 100,000 Bpd of Shale Oil," Report No. 75-4A, U.S. Bureau of Mines 1975.
[c]"Commercial Evaluation of an Oil Shale Industry Based on the Paraho Process," Harry Pforzyeimer, Paraho Development Corp. Presented at the 11th Israel Conference on Mechanical Engineering, July 11-12, 1977, Haifa, Israel.
[d]"Modifications to the Detailed Development Plan for Colorado C_b Tract," submitted by Ashland Oil Co., 1977.
[e]Paper presented by SAI at the 11th Annual Oil Shale Symposium, April 12-14, 1978, Golden Colo.
[f]Adapted From "An Economic Analysis of an Oil Shale, Nahcolite and Dawsonite Complex in Colorado, Option III,"U.S. Bureau of Mines, March 1974.
[g]"Evaluation of Combined in Situ and Surface Reporting of Oil Shale on Tract C_b," Shell Oil Co., Houston, Texas. Report prepared for U.S. Department of Interior, Bu Mines, November 1976.
[h]Includes operating costs for mineral recovery.
[i]Extrapolated values.

Low-Btu Coal Gasification. At least nine processes are commercially available for the production of low-Btu gas from coal for industrial applications. There are at least seven commercial users operating today in the United States. In addition, the Department of Energy has funded other promising concepts for low-Btu gas generation.

Potential applications where low- or medium-Btu gas might replace oil and natural gas include electric power generation as boiler fuel for existing oil or natural-gas fired utility boilers (retrofitting of existing steam boilers);

boiler fuel for new base-load service electric generating station boilers; and gas turbine fuel for combined cycle power plants in base-load and intermediate service.

Industrial fuel applications are boiler fuel for existing oil or natural-gas-fired boilers to generate process steam; steam raising; furnace kiln and oven fuel for process heat; and direct and indirect heating or space heating applications.

The industrial nonfuel applications include reducing gas for process metallurgy and ore reduction, and synthesis gas for chemical feed-stock and methanol production.

There are, however, several constraints to the use of low-Btu gasification systems in the industrial sector. Because this gas cannot be economically stored or transmitted over appreciable distances, coal would have to be shipped to gasification units near the points of consumption. (see tables 4–2 and 4–3).

Oil Shale. Tapping the Nation's tremendous shale oil resources to supplement petroleum supplies has long been a national goal because it represents a potential source of relatively secure oil and gas which can be drawn upon for several hundred years.

The principal deterrents to commercial shale oil production in this country are the lack of economic incentive and important environmental concerns. The risk-reward relationship does not appear favorable enough to

Table 4–2

Estimated Annual Production of Synthetic Gas and Liquids from Coal, 1985–2000

(quadrillion Btu)

Product	1985	1990	2000
Gas			
Low-Btu	0.2	0.2	1.3
Medium-Btu	.1	1.1	2.4
High-Btu	.2	.6	2.2
Liquids			
Boiler fuel	0	.4	1.4
Gasoline	.1	.3	1.4
Total	.6	2.6	8.7
CRS demand estimates	95.0	109.0	140.0

Source: Data derived from Draft DOE Commercialization Strategy Reports (TID 28846, 28849–51); assumes the federal government takes the necessary action to stimulate development.

Source for CRS demand estimates: Kaufman, Alvin, Warren Farb, and Barbara Daly. "U.S. Energy Demand Forecast, 1976–90," in *Project Independence: U.S. and World Energy Outlook Through 1990,* U.S. Senate Committee on Energy and Natural Resources.

Table 4–3
Estimated Capital Requirements for a Synthetic Fuel Industry, 1985–2000
(millions of 1978 dollars)

Type of Plant	1985	1990	2000
Gasification			
Low-Btu	$ 120	$ 1,800	$10,000
Medium-Btu	800	8,000	18,000
High-Btu	3,500	12,000	45,000
Liquefaction			
Boiler fuel	4	508	1,778
Gasoline	315	945	4,410
Total	4,739	23,253	79,188

Source: Based on data in DOE Commercialization Strategy Reports (TID 28846, 28849, 28850, 28851). Capital estimates assume the federal government takes the necessary action to stimulate development.

attract venture capital in the large amounts needed, unless additional incentives are provided, and uncertainties about shale oil's access to free markets are resolved.

With regard to the siting of oil shale plants, three counties in Colorado appear to be available to support an industry of 200,000 barrels per day. The Water Resources Council estimates that there is sufficient undedicated surface water to support shale oil production of 1.3 million barrels per day.

There are numerous processes available for the production of oil shale, and almost every major oil company is known to be interested in the conversion of shale.

While estimates of the cost of producing a barrel of shale oil vary considerably and appear to be particularly susceptible to inflationary pressure, table 4-1, prepared by the Laramie Energy Research Center gives a good idea of the price of oil produced by various technologies.

It is generally agreed that oil shale is probably our cheapest synthetic liquid fuel option. According to testimony presented before the Senate Subcommittte on Minerals, Materials and Fuels in November, 1976, by Dr. Philip C. White, Assistant Administrator for Fossil Energy, ERDA; "Oil shale production is closer to commercial acceptance than other liquid fuel alternatives."

However, these technologies have not been demonstrated yet on any significant scale. For example, the Paraho semi-works plant is only 150-200 barrels per day in size. This plant has produced, over time, 100,000 barrels which were subsequently refined. DOE recently released an RFP for an oil shale demonstration plant to be no larger than 10,000 barrels per day. It hopes to award this contract by the end of this year and to complete design by the end of next year. One of the applicants has recently testified that on an accelerated schedule they could construct that plant in two years and could have a commercial plant in operation by 1985.

One legitimate and unavoidable problem is evolving federal regulation under recently enacted environmental laws. New source performance standards for synfuel technologies will require the best available control technology standard. The Toxic Substances Control Act will control the product and most likely the wastes form liquid plants. The most likely impact will be strict regulations to control shipment. The Resource Conservation and Recovery Act may result in portions of the wastes from liquids plants being classified as hazardous, resulting in increased cost of disposal.

Summary. It cannot be assumed that every process that is carried to full-scale demonstration will prove to be fully acceptable. However, since a primary goal of national energy policy should be to develop the broad industrial base for the large scale production of synthetic fuels sufficient to meet the national production goal, it would seem necessary to build and operate at least one full-scale plant using each of the processes that appears promising after careful piloting and small-scale demonstration.

Ordinarily a full-scale plant would have to be equivalent in size and capacity to a full-scale production module (typically capable of about 20,000 to 50,000 barrels a day of production), and it would have to be operated on a full production schedule for a sufficiently long period of time (several years) to establish its costs, reliability, and any other factors needed to determine the commercial feasibility of a synthetic fuel process. However, in a period of insufficient or unreliable energy supplies, as we face today, it becomes a matter of national priority that a synthetic fuel capability be developed within the United States.

To maintain a high state of readiness in synfuels with respect to national security, we must allow at least 10 years lead time to have plants of some size in operation. Having conceptual designs ready will not accomplish this in view of the long lead-times for engineering, procurement, and construction. (Senate Publication 96–17, pp. 147–148).

Production Goals. If the federal government takes the necessary action to stimulate development of synthetic fuels, the estimated annual production of synthetic coal gases and liquids could be 600,000 barrels of oil equivalent per day by 1985, 2.6 million barrels by 1990 and 8.7 million barrels by the year 2000 (See table 4–2). The basic question, however, is whether or not synfuels can compete against other sources, especially when environmental costs are factored into the comparison.

Capital Requirements. A principal obstacle to the commercialization of synthetic fuels is the scale of the capital required. The Senate Budget Committee notes that in 1975 only 162 industrial corporations had assets greater than $1 billion, and only 30 had assets over $4 billion. It concluded that major oil firms and utilities are the most likely participants in synfuel ventures, although various manufacturing companies and smaller oil and coal companies have expressed interest. A major consortium would have to be assembled to spread risk adequately.

Moreover, some potential participants in synfuel development face particular financial constraints. Electric utilities, for example, are having difficulty raising capital for construction of new generating plants.

In 1975, only ten regulated natural gas utility companies had net plant and stockholder equities greater than $1 billion. The largest, Columbia Gas, had plant assets of only $1.063 billion. Such regulated companies will face great difficulty financing synthetic fuels such as coal gasification without federal incentives.

The estimated annual capital requirements would be $4.7 billion in 1985, $23.2 billion in 1990 and $79.1 billion in the year 2000 (See table 4-3.) This compares to a nonresidential fixed investment in 1978 dollars estimated at $285 billion in 1985, and between $280 billion and $337 billion in 1990. Thus the average annual investment required for all synfuel plants is only 0.2 percent of the nonresidential fixed investment in 1985 and 1.2 percent in 1990. As a consequence, funds should be available for the industry if the projects are deemed creditworthy by investors. In any case, the gas industry now spends over $2 billion a year for production and transmission construction alone, indicating that the synfuel capital is not out of line with traditional expenditures.

In the Omnibus Energy Act of 1980, synthetic fuels legislation, Congress rejected a 2.5 mboed (million barrel of oil equivalent per day) goal by 1990 and the attendant $88 billion federal commitment provided in the Administrations's Energy Security Corporation.

Instead, Congress proposed a goal of 1.5 mboed by 1995 with a committment to spend $20 billion through a federal Synthetic Fuels Corporation. The committees responsible for preparation of the Act argued that development of synthetic fuels on as rapid a schedule as that advocated by the Carter Administration would be impossible due to (1) technological uncertainties; (2) high costs; (3) capacity problems and (4) adverse environmental and socio-economic impacts.[12] This writer's view is that only the last objection is both empirically based and significant: It is, in effect, an objection to the following effects of the hasty Carter crash program proposal: 800 square miles of strip mining in Colorado, Utah, and Wyoming, where land reclamation is very difficult; oil shale waste greater in volume than the raw shale used (requiring filling estimated by the Committee on Environmental Quality, whose testimony the Senate accepts, to necessarily include canyon lands and wildlife habitats); water availability in those areas, sufficient to supply only a 500,000 boed oil shale industry, or alternatively, estimated to be sufficient to support oil shale production of 1.3 mboed, according to testimony of the Water Resource Council. The water requirement for synfuels production arises mainly from the need for cooling water to dispose of waste heat and the chemical used for hydrogen in the conversion process with raw shale. Mining of the shale requires further water.

Still, the committees' concern that the technology cannot be developed as fast as the Carter plan assumed, coupled with conflicting evidence about the ability to minimize adverse environmental effects, suggest that the 1980 act is a well-reasoned synthetic fuels strategy, which could always be expanded, as solutions to such problems are found. By 1985 it will be time to reassess progress.[13]

Conservation

The most striking aspect of the energy conservation program proposed by the 1980 Energy Act is that it includes no mandatory conservation measures. Of course, mandatory new car fuel economy standards already exist, under other authority. Synfuels efforts cannot have a significant impact on America's energy dependence in the near-term. Neither can solar energy (see following section). A vigorous effort to back foreign oil out of our economy is, therefore, a needed and complementary endeavor to a synfuels program. The conservation measures created by the 1980 Act, a paradigm of American government methodology, are laudable but too little.

Many witnesses testifying on energy measures have agreed that conservation is virtually the only energy resource available in quantities sufficient to make significant gains in improving our supply and demand situation through the early 1980s. It also appears to be available at very competitive prices. The recent Havard Business School study has estimated that 25 to 50 percent savings are available in American houses by improving the efficiency of space heating and cooling.[14] A recent study of the Princeton Center for Energy and Environmental Studies has shown that a combination of measures involving added insulation, caulking and weatherization, window improvements, and furnace modifications could save a typical resident 50 percent to 75 percent in fuel costs without loss of comfort.

The Harvard Business School study concluded that the United States can reduce its energy use 30 or 40 percent if concerted attention is given to exploiting energy conservation as a readily available energy resource.

The Conservation Bank established by the 1980 Energy Act provides long-term graduated repayment conservation loans of up to $2,500 per residence for 14 million households at up to 6 percent below market interest rates—this would be in addition to the current 15 percent tax credit qualifying energy conservation measures enjoy. It is a marvel of American consensus politics. That is, fearful of being accused of sponsoring a welfare program (out-right conservation grants as advocated by Senators Kennedy and Durkin) and equally fearful that mandatory measures smack of socialist compulsion, the Senate Banking Committee did what most Americans would expect (and desire) of it: it created a new bank,

Unfortunately, the Conservation Bank aims to do too little: it subsidizes loans to retrofit 14 million residences (houses plus apartments). Furthermore, it is purely voluntary. Although Americans would react against mandatory retrofitting, there are situations in which they would accept it, particularly in the sale of houses and building of new houses.

Although the 1980 act provides additional authority and funding for training auditors who perform energy audits pursuant to Section 215 of the National Energy Conservation Policy Act of 1978, it still does not amend the law to mandate that homeowners have an energy audit when selling their homes or that an audit be required on the sale of new homes. In a society historically as mobile as the United States, where one in every ten families moves each year, such a requirement (more coercive than a purely voluntary scheme but hardly oppressive) could have significant effect within a decade. Indeed, such a requirement is consistent with fair disclosure norms applicable to sale of homes in many states.[15]

The proposed model legislation (appendix 4B) improves upon the 1980 Act by requiring an energy audit (in terms that DOE would standardize and publicize) upon sale or exchange of any residence. Cost would be borne jointly be the effected utility companies and the Conservation Bank. New structures must comply with DOE standards under the National Energy Conservation Policy Act of 1978. The Conservation Bank would be authorized to provide loan subsidies to enable other structures to be brought up to standard. The term would be equal to the mortgage term, with no conservation loan downpayment and principal not included in the mortgage to income ratio computation made by the mortgage applicant's bank. Interest would be subsidized as under the 1980 Act. Maximum conservation loans are set at $3,000 in 1980 dollars, adjusted according to the housing component of the CPI. Resale of a house would require a new audit, repayment of the old conservation loan, and would qualify the house for a new loan (to pick up the balance of the old loan and avoid upward pressure on housing prices which would otherwise occur, or for new conservation measures needed to meet DOE standards).

Solar Energy

Again the Senate Banking Committee created a bank: The Solar Energy Bank. Before discussing it, existing solar energy programs need to be summarized.

Since 1974, twenty-two states have passed laws exempting solar equipment from state taxes or offering income tax incentives to homeowners and businesses installing solar heating systems. Twenty-seven states have laws reducing the amount of increased property taxes resulting from installing solar heating devices.

Federal programs have been focused primarily on research and development of solar (and other nenrenewable) technologies and the development of standards and certification procedures for solar systems. In late 1978, Congress enacted the National Energy Act which established several federal programs to provide financial incentives for installation of solar energy equipment. The financial incentives include a nonrefundable income tax credit for individuals who install solar energy devices in their principal residences; a business tax credit for solar investment; and a $100 million subsidized loan program for installation of solar devices in one to four-family residential structures.

The tax credits provided in the 1978 National Energy Act are under-utilized and generally not attractive to homeowners in the lower income brackets, and existing loan subsidy programs are also too narrow.

Like the Consevation Bank, the Solar Bank, created by Title II of the 1980 Energy Act, subsidizes the interest rate (up to 6 percent below market rate) made for installations of solar units. The bill authorizes sufficient money to fund subsidies for loans for 200,000 single-family houses. With an average loan size of $4,500, solar energy will remain the energy-source of the rich.

However, the 1980 Energy Act also requires that, where cost-effective, the federal government must use solar energy in construction, rehabilitation or long term lease of civilian federal buildings.[16] In light of this, it is curious (given that the Solar Bank is created within HUD) that the Banking Committee did not carry the thought to its logical conclusion: any buildings built with HUD loan subsidies or HUD backing of any kind must use solar energy where cost-effective. Such a provision would help plug the gap between lack of solar programs for low and middle income groups and federal solar assistance to upper income groups. The amendment to the Act in (appendix 4C) does just this.

Notes

1. 1976 Democratic Party Platform.

2. Richard J. Barnet, *The Lean Years, Politics In The Age Of Scarcity,* (New York: Simon and Schuster, 1980) at 21.

3. *There Are Alternatives: A Program For Controlling Inflation In The Necessities of Life,* Consumers Opposed To Inflation In the Necessities (1979) at 22 (mimeograph).

4. "Mandatory Energy Conservation and Gasoline and Diesel Fuel Rationing Part 1," Hearing Before the Subcommittee on Energy Regulation of the Committee on Energy and Natural Resources, United States Senate, 96th Congress, First Session, February 5, 1979 (hereinafter Rationing Hearings Part 1), p.53

5. Id.

6. T. Scitovsky, "The Political Economy of Consumers' Rationing", 24 *Review of Economic Statistics,* 114–115, (August 1942).

7. Salant, Walter S. "Rationing and Price as Methods of Restricting Demand for Specific Products," *Economics and Human Welfare,* Michael Boskin, ed. Academic Press, 1979.

8. Senate Committee on Energy and Natural Resources, statement of Chairman.

9. Report of Senate Energy Committee on Synthetic Fuels Act of 1975.

10. C.B.O. Study, January 1976.

11. C.B.O. Study, September 1979.

12. Extending The Defense Production Act of 1950, As Amended, Report of the Committee on Banking, Housing, and Urban Affairs and Energy and Natural Resources, United States Senate, together with Additional Supplemental and Minority Views, to accompany S932, October 30, 1979 (and hearings referred to therein).

13. Professor Mel Horwitch of the Harvard Business School Energy Project:

> The historical track record in synthetic fuels—of grandiose schemes and attractive technological and economic promises, followed by disappointment and dramatically rising cost estimates—should give us pause at this time when we are presented with the most ambitious proposals for synthetic fuels ever encountered in the United States... A massive synthetic fuels program is an example of choosing a conceptually simple technocratic solution for what is a complex societal problem...

U.S. Senate, Report on S.932, Government Printing Office, Washington, D.C. 1980, at 25–2.

14. *Energy Future,* Report of the Harvard Business School Energy Project (1979).

15. For example, Chapter 93A, Massachusetts General Laws.

16. Liberally defined to mean competitive with oil purchased, transported and refined at marginal international prices, discounted at 3 percent over the life of the equipment or 30 years whichever is less.

Appendix 4A:
A Model Act for
Mandatory
Conservation of
Gasoline and
Diesel Fuel

Notwithstanding any other provisions of law, the President shall work with the Department of Energy to implement within 90 days a stand-by mandatory plan of gasoline and diesel fuel conservation. The objectives of the plan shall be to reduce crude oil imports into the United States within 1 year of the date of implementation, by a percentage determined by the President and set forth in the National Energy Policy Plan in accordance with the terms of Title VIII of the Department of Energy Organization Act of 1977 and to minimize the disruptive effects on the U.S. economy of sudden and sharp increases in the price of imported oil.

The Department of Energy shall equitably allocate gasoline and diesel fuel among the states taking into account particular hardships caused by disproportionate automobile usage in the various states and Standard Metropolitan Statistical Areas within states. (Each state shall determine the method of allocating gasoline within its borders subject to the proviso that gasoline and diesel fuel must be made available for necessity use as detemined by the state in concert with the Department of Energy at prices in effect on October 1, 198__, while prices for non-necessity use may vary above such levels).

The President is encouraged to submit to the Congress a two-stage mandatory rationing plan. The first stage shall mandatorily allocate gasoline and diesel fuel, in response to an increase in the price of imported oil of more than 25% as compared with prices one year before, by means of negotiable ration coupons equitably allocated (as determined by state authorities in cooperation with the Department of Energy). As soon as is practicable, coupon rationing shall be superceded by a plan of excise-tax rationing, through which the excise tax is set to maintain the pattern of use of gasoline and diesel fuel established in the first stage, and proceeds of the excise tax equitably redistributed through tax credits and transfer payments to consumers of gasoline and diesel fuel.

At any time the President may terminate or otherwise modify the plan in a manner not inconsistent with the purposes of this Act.

Appendix 4B: Amendments to the Energy Act of 1980, Title IV— Conservation Bank

The Energy Act of 1980 is amended by adding the following subtitle to Title IV thereof:

Subtitle K — Mandatory Energy Audit Upon Sale or Exchange of Residence, Additional Energy Conservation Loan Authority.

(a) Prior to completion of the sale or exchange of any residential dwelling unit, a residential energy audit as herein above provided shall be conducted under penalty of law as herein provided. Failure of seller to have qualified auditor perform such audit (unless excused by the Department of Energy) shall not void any sale or exchange but shall provide a right of action for buyer against seller for failure to perform such audit prior to exchange for twice the reasonable cost of such audit and reasonable attorneys fees. Any seller not providing results of such audit to buyer shall be liable to the Department of Energy in civil suit for the reasonable cost of such audit. For willful violation of this section any person may be subject to a fine of $5,000 or imprisonment for not longer than five years or both.

(b) No residential dwelling not in compliance with standards of residential efficiency promulgated by the Department of Energy pursuant to the National Energy Conservation Policy Act of 1978 may be sold or exchanged unless

    (i) an energy audit as required in subparagraph (a) of this subtitle has been performed; and

    (ii) an undertaking has been made by seller to make repairs or alterations necessary to bring such dwelling unit into compliance with such standards prior to sale, or buyer has filed with the Conservation Bank or any bank or other lending agency acting on its behalf a plan to make repairs or alterations necessary to bring such dwelling unit into compliance with such standards within three years of the date of sale or exchange.

(c) For the purpose of assisting purchasers of dwelling units in making the repairs or alterations required by this subtitle, the Conservation Bank shall make loans to such purchasers, directly or acting through intermediary lending institutions upon the following terms:

    (i) a satisfactory report of a qualified energy auditor is filed prior to purchase;

    (ii) a plan for making changes or alterations necessary to enable that dwelling unit to conform to Department of Energy standards has been filed;

    (iii) in no case shall the Conservation Bank lend or subsidize the loan of more than $3,000 per single family dwelling unit in 1980 dollars adjusted according to the rate of increase in the housing component of the Consumer Price Index;

    (iv) in no case shall the Conservation Bank subsidize qualifying loans to an extent greater than 6% below prevailing market rates;

(v) the Conservation Bank or its intermediaries shall conduct periodic audits to assure compliance with these terms and implementation of residential energy plans for which loans are provided.

(d) There are appropriated such sums as shall be necessary to carry out the objectives of this subtitle.

Appendix 4C:
HUD Solar Energy
Amendment

Section 706 of the Energy Act of 1980 is amended by adding the following subsections:

(k) Effective one hundred and eighty days after the date of enactment of this title, all construction, reconstruction or renovation projects assisted by the Department of Housing and Urban Development shall include to the maximum extent practicable, inclusion of, or the use of, cost effective solar energy systems.

(l) For the purposes of this section "projects" includes any form of federal assistance to building, reconstruction or renovation under the direction, supervision or authority of the Department of Housing and Urban Development.

(m) The Solar Bank shall make such money available to the Secretary, upon terms and conditions not inconsistent with that made available by the Solar Bank to other persons, in order to assist in the financing of Solar energy systems included or used in projects as required by subsection (k) of this section.

5 Housing

The central role of the housing sector in any strategy to break the cycles of inflation and recession is clear. In a largely unconstrained financial system, only very large increases in interest rates can slow credit expansion. But such increases (of six or more points in the prime rate within two months) lead to "disintermediation"—withdrawal of savers' money from thrift institutions in favor of money-market funds. This has a devastating effect on the housing industry as mortgage money dries up forcing the industry into a cyclical downturn, followed by a cyclical decline in production of the myriad products that depend on housing. In 1980, housing starts plummeted to an annualized rate of slightly more than 1 million starts. Over 2 million starts is generally considered the minimum necessary to avoid worsening America's excess demand for housing. As previously noted, during the 1971–1972 wage-price control program housing starts exceeded 2 million annually. This chapter presents three proposals to use existing legislation to increase availability of mortgage money for necessity housing, whenever annual housing starts fall below the 2 million level. These proposals aim to check the cyclical downturn from becoming extreme.

The first idea, special reserve requirements on mortgage assets to expand mortgage lending for necessity housing, was developed by the National Center for Economic Alternatives and the Public Interest Research Group of Washington, D.C. The second idea was suggested by Rudy Oswald, Research Director AFL–CIO. It is that mutual funds and money market funds dedicate an increasing percentage of their portfolios to mortgage lenders when annualized housing starts dip below 2 million units. I have taken that suggestion to imply that since Federal Reserve tight-money policies typically result in savers withdrawing funds from savings banks in favor of money market funds, such funds should be required to lend a scheduled percentage of new funds received under such circumstances to mortgage lenders in order to partially offset the drying-up of mortgage money occassioned by a switch of funds from savings banks to money market funds. The third idea, called equity-sharing, relies on the private sector with federal insurance and may have the greatest potential for easing inflation in the cost of housing. Under equity-sharing, a mortgagor's interest rate is reduced, by one-third for instance, if he agrees to give up one-third of the capital appreciation to the bank upon sale of the house.

The first two proposals make use of the Credit Control Act of 1969.[1]

121

Special Reserve Requirements on Mortgage Assets to
Lower Mortgage Rates for Necessity Housing

The inflationary impact on high mortgage rates could be offset, to a significant extent, by using a system of reserve requirements on mortgage assets to lower the mortgage rate for low, moderate, and middle priced housing (necessity) and raise the mortgage rate for high priced housing (luxury). Such a system would provide immediate relief in the form of lower mortgage rates to the majority of home purchasers. Moreover, it would result in an immediate and substantial reduction in the Consumer Price Index. In measuring home prices, the CPI currently focuses on the price of necessity housing and excludes the price of luxury housing. If mortgage rates are lowered for necessity housing and raised for luxury housing, it would likewise be appropriate for the CPI to register only the lower rates for necessity housing. Under this approach, lowering the necessity mortgage rate from 10 percent to 9 percent (a 10 percent decline) would reduce the CPI by 0.73 percent—a reduction far beyond that which can be achieved by trimming the federal budget or employing voluntary wage-price guidelines.

Higher mortgage rates for luxury housing should produce another immediate inflation reduction benefit by dampening the demand for high priced homes. Dampened demand for luxury housing should lower prices of both luxury and necessity housing, since the recent escalation of prices for high priced homes has exerted strong upward pressure on the price of necessity housing. If in fact higher mortgage rates do not significantly curb the demand for luxury housing, then the mortgage asset reserve requirements can be coupled with more restrictive down-payment and maturity period requirements for luxury mortgage loans.

Opening a gap between necessity and luxury mortgage rates will also generate another anti-inflation benefit. Lower necessity rates will increase the demand for construction of new moderately priced homes, while higher luxury rates are curbing the demand for new high priced homes. This shift in production will lower the average price of new homes. In fact, such a spread between necessity and luxury mortgage rates is necessary to offset some of the undesirable housing production effects of the federal income tax deduction for mortgage interest. This deduction allows upper income persons purchasing luxury housing to pay effective mortgage rates that are substantially below those paid by low, moderate, and middle income persons. The result is overproduction of luxury housing and underproduction of necessity housing.

A necessity-luxury mortgage rate spread will increase the overall production of new homes. Since the demand for necessity housing is far more interest rate-elastic than the demand for luxury housing, the new necessity housing stimulated by lower necessity mortgage rates will greatly exceed the decline in luxury housing resulting in higher luxury rates. The resulting new increase in home production will have an intermediate-term anti-inflation effect.

Finally, a necessity-luxury mortgage rate spread is warranted as a matter of equity. The inequity inherent in lower tax-adjusted mortgage rates for upper income persons has produced a major impetus to the growing use by state and local governments of tax-exempt bond issues to provide lower rate mortgages to middle as well as lower income persons.

Establishing special reserve requirements for mortgage loans provides the vehicle for lowering mortgage rates for necessity housing and raising mortgage rates for luxury housing. Each institutional mortgage lender would be required to maintain mortgage reserves equal to a fixed percentage of its mortgage loans originations. These mortgage reserves would be held by the Federal Home Loan Bank System (FHLB) and would be entirely separate from the reserves on deposit liabilities that commercial banks maintain with the Federal Reserve System. The mortgage reserves can be used in either of two alternative ways to shift the lender's yield downward. One approach is for the FHLB System to pay lenders a high rate of interest on reserves for necessity mortgage loans and no interest on reserves for luxury loans. The other approach is to pay no interest on reserves, impose mortgage-asset reserve requirements only for luxury mortgages, and give mortgage lenders a reserve credit for necessity mortgages that would reduce their required reserves for luxury mortgages. In either case competition would force lenders to offer the high-yield necessity mortgages at lower market rates and the low-yield luxury mortgages at high market rates. Under either approach it should be feasible to lower necessity mortgage interest rates 1 percent below market rate, for instance from 10.5 percent to 9.5 percent, and to raise luxury mortgage rates 1 percent above market rate, from 10.5 percent to 11.5 percent.

Defining Necessity and Luxury Housing for the Mortgage Reserve Requirements

Necessity housing should be defined broadly to include housing purchased by lower, moderate, and middle income persons. If necessity housing is defined broadly then nonnecessity housing can properly be viewed as luxury housing. A possible approach would be to consider all single family homes, both new and existing, with a sale price of $75,000 or less as necessity housing. At current price levels roughly 80 percent of all existing homes sold and roughly 70 percent of all new homes sold have prices of $75,000 or less (see tables 5-1 and 5-2).

Second homes should be viewed as luxury housing, regardless of their

Table 5-1
Sales Price Distribution of New and Existing Single-Family Homes

	Existing Homes (December 1978)	New Homes (4th quarter, 1978)
Average sale price (mean)	$58,100	$66,400
Median sale price	$50,900	$59,000
$ 75,000 or more	20%	30%
$ 85,000 or more	15%	20%
$100,000 or more	9%	11%

Source: Public Interest Research Group.

Table 5-2
Production and Sales of Single-Family Homes—1978

Private home starts	1,433,000
New homes sold	818,000
Existing homes sold	3,905,000

Source: Public Interest Research Group.

purchase price. Second homes, used primarily for recreational purposes, represent a growing share of single family homes. Census Bureau data indicate that second homes represent from 3.4 percent to 5.1 percent of the nation's 80 million housing units and suggest that the great majority of these are single family structures. If these 3 to 4 million single family homes turn over at the same 7 percent annual rate as other single family homes, then as many as 280,000 existing second homes are sold each year. As for construction of new second homes, the National Association of Home Builders has estimated that as many as 150,000 new second homes are produced each year.

If necessity housing is defined as all single family homes priced at $75,000 or less (excluding all second homes, and including multi-family, low-to-moderate income co-operatives), then regional variation in sale prices becomes a major issue. In high-priced housing areas a smaller than average proportion of home sales will qualify as necessity housing and be eligible for lower rate mortgage loans, while a larger than average proportion will be defined as luxury and face higher mortgage rates. Taking the extreme cases, in San Francisco and Washington, D.C. the 1980 median sale price was above $80,000 for existing homes and $90,000 for new homes. Under a $75,000 ceiling for necessity homes, only about 45 percent of existing homes and 25 percent of new homes in the SMSAs would qualify as necessity, as opposed to the 1980 national averages of 80 percent and 70 percent respectively.

One solution to this problem would be a sliding ceiling for defining necessity housing in each SMSA or other geographic area that would be equal to the price level at which 80 percent of the SMSA's existing homes are sold. However, such a strict geographic parity approach would be somewhat self-defeating since it would reward areas that failed to build moderate priced housing with a more lax standard. A better solution would be a minimum requirement that at least 50 percent of existing home sales qualify as necessity housing. In an SMSA where the median sale price for existing homes is above $75,000—that is, less than 30 percent of existing sales qualify as necessity housing under the $75,000 ceiling—the definition of necessity housing would be raised to the median sale price. At present it seems that only Washington, D.C., San Francisco, Los Angeles, and possibly San Diego have median sale prices on existing homes above $75,000. Thus a 50 percent minimum eligibility requirement could be easily administered since it requires anlysis of sale price data in only a few areas.

Mortgage Reserves

A mortgage reserve requirement for a particular type of mortgage shifts the lender's yield on that type of mortgage. The extent of this yield shift depends on the size of the reserve requirement—for example, 10 percent or 15 percent of the mortgage amount—and the rate of interest that the lender receives on the reserves—for instance, no interest or 10 percent interest.

A reasonable goal for mortgage reserves would be to lower the mortgage rate on necessity loans by 1 percent (100 base points) and to raise the rate on luxury loans by 1 percent (100 base points). At recent market rates this would result in roughly a 9.5 percent necessity rate and a 11.5 luxury rate. It is also possible to seek a graduated structure of mortgage rates by subdividing the necessity and the luxury sectors into subsectors with different reserve requirements. For example, possible targets would be to raise the mortgage rate 1 percent (100 base points) on $75,000 to $90,000 homes and 1.5 percent (150 base points) on homes over $90,000.

Since the purpose of the reserves is to influence the lender's yield on new mortgage loans, mortgage originations provide a better basis for calculating reserve requirements than mortgage loans outstanding or changes in the level of mortgages outstanding. Thus, the reserve requirement should attach to a mortgage loan at the time of origination and continue for several years. The requirement should be imposed on the outstanding balance of the mortgage. If the mortgage is transferred from one lender to another the reserve requirement would follow the mortgage.

Differential Interest Payment Approach

A spread between necessity and luxury mortgage rates can be established by either of two alternative reserve techniques: imposing uniform reserve requirements on all necessity and luxury mortgage loans and paying a high rate of interest on necessity reserves and no interest on luxury reserves, or imposing reserve requirements on luxury mortgages and providing reserve credits for necessity mortgages.

Existing Statutory Authority to Establish a Mortgage
Reserve System

The Credit Control Act of 1969 (12. U.S.C. 1901 *et seq.)* authorizes the president to direct the Federal Reserve Board to establish credit controls for the purpose of controlling inflation. The act also authorizes the Federal Reserve Board to use the services of other federal agencies in establishing credit controls.This law provides statutory authority for the president to direct the Federal Reserve Board to direct the Federal Home Loan Bank System to establish mortgage reserve requirements.

Mortgage reserve requirements will have a major impact in moderating inflation in the housing sector and thus are within the intended scope of the Credit Control Act. Sec. 205 (a) of the act provides authority to regulate or control all extensions of credit. Section 206 (7), after specifically authorizing particular limitations on loan terms, goes on to authorize: "any other specifications...of the...conditions of any extension of credit." Requiring reserves for mortgage loans is a specification of the conditions of extending mortgage credit.

The act's legislative history reinforces the broad statutory language. According to the House managers for the Senate-House Conference, Congress intended that:

> the President would be afforded the broadest possible spectrum of alternatives in fighting inflation, curbing unnecessary extensions of credit, and channeling credit into housing or other essential purposes.[2]

Rather than new legislation, if any congressional action were thought desirable to implement such a system, a joint resolution such as the example in appendix 5A might be appropriate. However, given the recent Senate action aimed at repealing the Credit Control Act of 1969, a proposed joint resolution seems an inadvisable approach. It might give the Senate opportunity to make a record against the proposal. Direct lobbying of the administration would seem preferable, even if no greater hope can be held for its success.

Portfolio Requirements for Investment Companies in Times of Severe Housing Slump

This proposal will be sketched in broadest outline as a vehicle for stimulating further discussion. The objective (and attendant danger) is clear. Money market funds and other investment funds into which money flows during periods of tight-money Federal Reserve Policy would be required to make increasing percentages of their new funds available to mortgage lenders. This would counterbalance the tendency of those funds to bid away assets from savings banks, diminishing the base upon which mortgages are made. The danger, of course, is that dictating the portfolio mix of such funds for whatever purpose is inconsistent with a free market. It permits the criticism that once allowed, other government-dictated objectives will be found for additional percentages of the funds' portfolios.

Nevertheless, the direct source of increase in money market assets following tight money policy changes, such as Paul Volker's October 1979 shift, is largely withdrawal of savings from savings banks—not entirely so since there is also significant shift from equity securities to money market certificates.

This proposal would have the Federal Reserve measure the extent of the shift from savings to money market funds, upon a rise in the Federal Reserve Rate, and require by way of adjustment that an increasing percentage of such new funds entering money market funds be lent to qualifying banks, such banks would be required to pay x percent of the current yield obtainable by the fund on the day the loan to the bank is made. Obviously x is a subject of political bargaining, but it would defeat the purpose of the proposal if it approached 100 percent. The clear social choice embodied in the proposal is in favor of a healthy, stabilized housing sector, and the social return from a healthy, stabilized housing sector is viewed as greater than the difference between x and 100 percent.

Finally, existing limits on savings bank interest could be eliminated, or suspended, during periods of tight-money, as an alternative to this plan. That would, however, generally raise mortgage rates to undesirable levels.

Again, a joint resolution (see appendix 5B) is a possible, although not necessarily currently advisable, approach.

Equity-Sharing—An Idea Whose Time Has Come

In 1980, a private investment bank in New York and a commercial bank in Florida experimented (without federal assistance) with a plan for equity-sharing mortgages. Under the scheme used there, home buyers were charged one-third less interest if they agreed to transfer one-third of the appreciation of the house upon eventual sale. Consumer response to the idea was overwhelming.

For example, a family could assume an 8 percent mortgage rather than a 12 percent mortgage on a $75,000 house (saving approximately $50,000 in interest charges over the life of the 30 year mortgage) by agreeing to give up one-third of the sale price of the house above $75,000. To the extent that the house appreciates more than three times the interest savings, the family is better off with the equity mortgage in absolute dollar terms. But since the interest savings begins immediately and the one-third equity appreciation give-up occurs later, when the house is sold, the house need not even appreciate by three times the interest savings, but only by three times its discounted present value. The bank gambles to some extent on the house and the neighborhood. But in an era of inflation, the bank is basically reducing the interest charge on the bet that the mortgaged house will appreciate in value at least as fast as the general long term rate of inflation as perceived on the date of the mortgage.

If the inflation rate turns out as expected but the house appreciates even faster, the bank makes out better than with a conventional mortgage. If the general inflation rate is greater than expected, traditionally the bank would lose out; the conventional mortgage rate is fixed. But equity-sharing gives the bank a way of recouping return on its fixed-rate loan otherwise lost to inflation higher than expected. Moreover, it allows the bank to do so without requiring a floating mortgage rate—an increasingly used mortgage method which unfortunately reduces homeowners' certainty. There is typically a limited proviso in the mortgage to give the bank a right of appraisal should it believe the sale of the house is at too low a price.

Equity-sharing has begun without federal help. It may flourish without it. If so, it offers the hope of a potentially dramatic check on housing costs. It is probably most attractive to the private sector as applied to newly built prime neighborhood homes. Certainly that could be a great stimulus to building, but it would not distribute equity sharing opportunities to purchasers of older homes in less than prime neighborhoods. Consequently, the federal role should be to encourage equity sharing in mortgages made for new homes and for existing housing in a range of neighborhoods. The Federal Home Loan Bank should be prompted to do so.

Notes

1. In June 1980, the U.S. Senate (but not the House) voted to repeal the Credit Control Act of 1969, 12 U.S.C. §1901 *et seq.*

2. Senate-House Conference Report No.91–769, December, 18, 1969.

Appendix 5A:
Joint Resolution—
Mortgage Reserve
System

Pursuant to the Credit Control Act of 1969, it is resolved that the Federal Reserve Board and the Federal Home Loan Bank Board establish a Mortgage Reserve System with the objective of lowering mortgage interest rates on necessity housing and correspondingly raising mortgage interest rates on luxury housing, thereby making more mortgage money available for purchase of necessity housing.

The Federal Reserve Board and the Federal Home Loan Bank Board shall adopt appropriate definitions of necessity and luxury housing and appropriate reserve requirements to accomplish this objective.

Appendix 5B:
Joint Resolution—
Portfolio Requirements

Pursuant to the Credit Control Act of 1969, it is resolved that the Federal Reserve Board and Federal Home Loan Bank shall establish a schedule of portfolio requirements which Investment Companies, registered under the Investment Company Act of 1940, 15 U.S.C. §§80a–1 to 80a–52, shall meet as to new investments made by such Companies from and after any date that the Federal Reserve Bank Board determines that annualized housing starts have fallen below the rate of 2 million per year.

Such portfolio requirements shall aim to increase the percentage of such Companies' investment portfolios invested directly or indirectly in the making of primary residence mortgages.

6   Health

This chapter presents a proposal for containing hospital costs that improves upon once proposed, and long since abandoned, mandatory cost-containment legislation.[1] More recent proposals offer only voluntary encouragement to hospitals to control costs.[2] The model legislation proposed in appendix 6A incorporates the best aspects of the abandoned mandatory bill amending it to incorporate strengths in a bill sponsored by Senator Talmadge at the time of the mandatory proposals.[3] The model act is set forth in appendix 6A.

Thirty years of expanding the hospital care system has led to great social gains but enormous social cost: hospital expenditures rose from $3.7 billion in 1950 to $55.4 billion in 1976, and are expected to surpass $100 billion in 1982.[4] Hospital costs increased from 1968 to 1978 at an annual rate of 15 percent.[5]

Mandatory hospital cost-containment proposals have aimed at slowing the rapid expansion of hospital sevices by setting a temporary limit on total hospital revenues and by decreasing and subjecting to govenmental approval capital outlays for new equipment and expanded or improved facilities. The Talmadge proposal aimed to accomplish another—complementary—objective: more efficient utilization of hospital resources. It did so by rewarding hospitals which deliver inexpensive care and by penalizing those which provide inordinately expensive care. This carrot and stick approach was backed up by a provision for aiding hospitals which suffered in the short-run from cutting back excess capacity.

The model legislation presented in appendix 6A marries the "capital outlay limit" and the "utilization oriented" bill into one mandatory bill that both controls capital expansion and provides utilization incentives. Thus, it is a joint capital outlay control, utilization incentive proposal.

Hospital costs are a rapidly increasing percentage of total health care costs and of U.S. GNP.[6] Between 1966 and 1980, federal funding of health costs exploded from $2.5 billion in 1966 (2.5 percent of the federal budget) to over $50 billion (12 percent of the federal budget).

There are at least four often cited reasons why pricing of health care costs in general and hospital costs in particular is not subject to the normal restraints of the market place: (1) because of the level of sophistication of medical knowledge, "consumer sovereignty" is largely replaced by physician controlled decision-making about what treatment is needed at what cost; (2) hospitals are typically oblivious to profit considerations (and, properly so), with the result that the system operates on an open-ended cost-plus basis; (3) third-party payers pay over 90 percent of all hospital bills [7] and (4) such third party payers pay based on the actual cost incurred rather than on a predetermined price schedule. [8]

Rather than maximizing profits, hospitals maximize growth (promotions, capital expansion) which often correlates with enhanced prestige. Third party payers' reimbursement for incurred costs does not provide an incentive to economize, to check these ambitions where prestige is too costly.

Mandatory Cost Control

Prudent cost control would place a ceiling on a hospital's total revenue and revenue per patient, coupled with a mechanism to assure that slower growth of hospital revenues is accompanied by greater efficiency in utilizing and purchasing hospital equipment. This would reduce the volume of unneeded treatment, but requires a delicate choice of the desirable growth rate (and, therefore, growth ceiling).

Translating these goals into practice is tricky because limitations on revenues (necessarily defined in terms of increases above a base year) could foster behavior on the part of hospital administrators aimed to maximize revenues without violating the revenue increase rule. Thus, for example, limits on revenues measured on a patient per diem basis (compared with the base year) would foster decreased per diem costs stretched over a longer hospital stay. Inducing extended hospitalization can be avoided by weighting the per diem revenue limit by a factor reflecting the ratio of current number of admissions to a moving average of past annual admissions. Then, hospitals that extend stays would not impermissably increase revenues in circumvention of the limit on revenues.

Revenues limits must allow at least for annual revenue increases (with the above-mentioned adjustments). What measure of annual inflation to allow for is itself important. The CPI or GNP implicit price deflators are less relevant indices of hospital cost increases than the American Hospital Association's "Hospital Input Price Index".

The extent, if any, to which adjusted revenue ceilings in a mandatory bill exceed increases in the Hospital Input Price Index must be the result of a political bargain. The mandatory bill proposed by Carter in 1977 (and later abandoned) chose an additional permissable revenue amount equal to one-third of the difference between the average annual rate of increase in a hospital's total hospital expenditures during the prior two years and the corresponding increase in the GNP price deflator. The model legislation appended here borrows Carter's one-third difference (as an example of one possible bargain) but replaces the GNP deflator with the HIPI, to give a more relevant, more precise, probably more restrictive comparison. Certain other adjustments are necessary to bring "base year" hospital revenues into line with the effective date of the bill. Thus some limit on anticipatory expansion of hospitals aware of impending mandatory cost control is required. The model bill, as did the Carter bill, limits such anticipatory expansion to 15 percent per year.

In addition, the bill calls for special scrutiny of major capital purchases (for example, above $150,000) by requiring a certificate of need.

An intelligent feature of the Carter proposal, retained in the model bill, is a certain stickiness downward in the revenue ceiling. This slowness in the decrease of the revenue limits, in situations where fewer patients are treated annually, encourages hospitals to focus increased hospital resources to each patient treated. Therefore, if a hospital's revenue ceiling remains constant despite as much as a 10 percent decrease in patients treated, hospitals are rewarded for minimizing treatment of patients not truly needing care, and freed-up to use such resource-savings on other patients. Moreover, decrease in patients treated not due to a shift away from unnecessary treatment but to a decline in service area population would be adjusted for by the moving average of past annual admissions adjustment previously mentioned. Enforcement of the revenue ceiling is accomplished through nonpayment of Medicare and Medicaid funds above the permitted ceiling, by an excise tax on payments made above the ceiling, and by HEW authority to take other measures (such as suspension from Medicare and Medicaid). The bill also provides for civil remedies in the event that prohibited expenditures are incurred.

Incentives for Increasing Utilization Efficiency

Revenue limits alone, even if they incorporate intelligent principles that discourage circumvention, and reflect sensible political bargains on the key formulas, will do little to foster increased efficiency in individual hospitals. The Talmadge proposal, referred to at the outset of this chapter, encouraged increased efficiency by establishing categorical standards by which hospital performance is evaluated and government reimbursement approved. To start with, standards would be established for the most routine (and easily measured) categories of care. Government reimbursement of hospital expenditures (such as for room and board) would be limited to 120 percent of the average cost of that category of treatment. High-cost hospitals are penalized by disallowance. Low-cost hospitals would be rewarded by being permitted a slightly higher allowable capital expansion rate. Such a scheme addresses a problem not solved by the Carter mandatory bill: a mandatory ceiling related to a hospital's "base period" unavoidably begins by rewarding inefficient hospitals (whose costs have been skyrocketing in and prior to the base year) while penalizing hospitals that have controlled their growth. The Talmadge scheme complements a scheme like Carter's because it addresses just such problems, among others. A further example of the two schemes' complementary nature is that a mandatory revenue ceiling, standing alone, does not encourage innovation, whereas a Talmadge-like scheme clearly does.

The appended model bill integrates the revenue ceiling and utilization efficiency ideas. It provides for development of categorical cost comparison data. It sets up a regulatory climate in which the rate of hospital expansion is, for the first time, made a matter of conscious social choice, but, at the same time, leaves hospitals free to choose the mix of resources each deems most efficient, with rewards and penalties for excessive deviation from the norm.

Among other things, review of the appendix will alert the reader to the complexity of the federal involvement required to control runaway hospital expenditures, and the need for vigorous local input to tailor the scheme to particular cases.

Notes

1. S.1391; H.R. 6575, 95th Cong., 1st Sess., introduced April 25, 1977.
2. *See, e.g.:* H.R. 2626, 96th Cong., 1st Sess., introduced November 15, 1979, and House Resolution 486, 96th Cong., 1st Sess., introduced November 14, 1979.
3. S.1470, 95th Cong., 1st Sess., introduced May 5, 1977. *See, generally:* "Hospital Cost Control: Single Edged Initiatives For A Two-Sided Problem," by Ronald Greenspan, Harvard Law School '79, 15 *Harvard Journal on Legislation* No. 3, pp. 603–668 (1978).
4. Gibson & Mueller, "National Health Expenditures, Fiscal Year 1976," 40 *Social Security Bulletin* 3, 15 (April 1977). Congressional Budget Office for the Subcomm. on Health and Scientific Research, 95th Cong., 1st Sess., *The Hospital Cost Containment Act of 1977: An Analysis of the Administration's Proposal* 13 (Comm. Print, 1977).
5. "Controlling Rising Hospital Costs", Congressional Budget Office, September 1979, Table 1.
6. Hospital costs account for approximately 4% of U.S. GNP and have doubled as a percentage of GNP in the past 12 years. By contrast, in Canada, hospital costs account for a relatively stable 3% of GNP. Over one-half of the increase in cost-per-patient-day since 1960 is attributable to

rising input prices and wage rates. Increased intensity of services comprises the remainder of the increase, with the nonlabor component accounting for four times the expenditure increase caused by the addition of personnel.

7. *Supra,* note 3.

8. *See generally:* Kenneth Arrow, "Uncertainty and the Welfare Economics of Medical Care," *American Economic Review,* 1963, pp. 941–973.

Appendix 6A:
Model Mandatory
Hospital Cost
Containment Act

To establish a system of hospital cost containment by providing for incentives and restraints to contain the rate of increase in hospital revenues, to provide for the development of permanent reforms in hospital reimbursement designed to provide incentives for the efficient and effective use of hospital resources, and for other purposes.

Be it enacted by the Senate and House of Representatives of the United States of America in Congress assembled,

SHORT TITLE

Section 1. This Act may be cited as the "Hospital Cost Containment Act of 198__."

REPORT ON PERMANENT REFORM IN THE DELIVERY AND FINANCING OF HEALTH CARE

Sec.2. The Secretary of Health and Human Services (hereinafter in this Act referred to as the "Secretary") shall submit to the Congress, no later than March 1, 198__, a report setting forth his recommendations for permanent reforms in the delivery and financing of health care which will increase the efficiency, effectiveness, and quality of health care in the United States and which will replace the transitional provisions of title I of this Act.

TITLE I—HOSPITAL COST CONSTRAINT PROVISIONS

Part A — Purpose and General Description of the Revenue Limit Program

PURPOSE

Sec. 101. It is the purpose of the hospital cost containment program established by this title to constrain the rate of increases in total acute care hospital inpatient costs, beginning July 1, 198__, and continuing until the adoption of the permanent reforms referred to in section 2, by limiting the amount of revenue which may be received, by the hospitals involved, from Government programs, private insurers, and individuals who pay directly for such care.

GENERAL DESCRIPTION OF REVENUE LIMIT PROGRAM

Sec. 102. (a) In order to carry out the purpose of the revenue limit program as set forth in section 101, the inpatient revenues of short-term acute care and specialty hospitals (excluding new hospitals and certain HMO-related hospitals) are to be limited in the manner outlined in the succeeding provisions of this section (and more particularly described in parts B and C of this title).

(b) The increase in total revenue which a hospital (as defined in section 121) may receive in any accounting year in the form of —

(1) reimbursement paid under the Medicare and Medicaid programs, and by cost payers, for inpatient services, and

(2) charges imposed upon other persons for inpatient services, may not, on a peradmission basis, exceed the average inpatient reimbursement due or inpatient charges imposed per inpatient admission in the base period (in general, the hospital's accounting year ending in 198__) by more than the percentage which is applicable to the hospital for such accounting year under section 111.

(c) Such percentage, in the case of any hospital for any accounting year, is to be determined by —

(1) establishing for such year, under section 112 (b), an "inpatient hospital revenue increase limit" based on increases in the Hospital Input Price Index and in total hospital expenditures nationwide.

(2) modifying the limit so established by the "admission load formula", as promulgated under section 113, to take account of major changes in patient loads experienced by that particular hospital, in order to arrive at an "adjusted inpatient hospital revenue increase limit" for that hospital in such year, and

(3) applying such adjusted limit for periods after June 30, 198__, with recognition being given under section 111(a) (1) to cost increases prior to that date.

(d) An exception from the limits otherwise established may be granted in accordance with section 115 (for a particular period) to any hospital which is experiencing substantially higher costs as a result of extraordinary changes in facilities and services, to the extent required to assure that the necessary additional revenue will be availabe where necessary to meet actual community needs.

(e) Compliance with these limits is to be enforced, in accordance with section 116, in various ways. Such compliance is required under the Medicare program by directly applying the limits for purposes of both interim and final reimbursement. Amounts paid to hospitals under the Medicaid program in excess of such limits will be disallowed as a basis for Federal matching payments. Hospitals and non-government cost payers exceeding the limits will be subject to a Federal excise tax in an amount equal to 150 per centum of the excess (except in the case of a hospital which is exempt as a result of corrective actions as prescribed under section 116(d) (2)).

(f) The Secretary is authorized, under section 117, to waive the limits otherwise established for all hospitals located in any State which has had in effect for at least one year a hospital cost containment program which covers at least 90 per centum of all acute care hospitals in the State, applies to all payers except the Medicare program, limits inpatient hospital revenue increases to a rate no greater (in the aggregate) than the rate established for the period involved under section 112(b), and provides for return of excess hospital revenues.

PART B — Establishment of Hospital Cost
Containment Program

IMPOSITION OF LIMIT ON HOSPITAL REVENUE INCREASES

Sec. 111. (a) The average reimbursement paid to a hospital for inpatient services under Title XVIII of the Social Security Act, under a State plan approved under

Title V or Title XIX of such Act, or by any cost payer, and the average charges imposed by a hospital for inpatient services, in any accounting year any part of which falls within a period subject to this title, may not (except as provided in subsection (b)) exceed the base inpatient hospital revenue per inpatient admission (as established under section 114) by a percentage greater than the sum of —

(1) the percentage by which the costs involved would have increased in the period elapsing after the close of the hospital's base accounting year and prior to July 1, 198__, if such costs had increased (during that period) at the average annual rate actually experienced by the hospital during the two-year period ending with the close of such base accounting year, except that such percentage as applied for purposes of this section shall not be more than 15 per centum nor less than 6 per centum,

(2) the percentage by which such costs would have increased in the period elapsing after June 30, 198__, and prior to the first day of the accounting year for which the limit is being imposed if such costs had increased (during such period) at an annual rate consistent with the inpatient hospital revenue increase limit determined and promulgated under section 112(b), and

(3) the percentage by which such costs would have increased in the accounting year for which the limit is being imposed if such costs had increased (during such year) at an annual rate consistent with the adjusted inpatient hospital revenue increase limit applicable to the hospital under section 112(a).

(b) Where less than a full accounting year falls within a twelve-month period subject to this title, the limit set forth in subsection (a) of this section, and the limit established under section 112(a), shall apply with respect to reimbursement due or charges imposed for the part of such accounting year which falls within such period in the same proportion as the number of days in such accounting year that fall within such period bears to the total number of days in such accounting year.

DETERMINATION OF ADJUSTED INPATIENT HOSPITAL
REVENUE INCREASE LIMIT

Sec. 112. (a) The "adjusted inpatient hospital revenue increase limit" which is applicable to any hospital for purposes of section 111 (a)(3) with respect to any accounting year shall (subject to section 111(b) and section 124) be equal to the inpatient hospital revenue increase limit determined and promulgated under subsection (b) of this section for the twelve-month period in which such an accounting year or any part thereof falls, modified by the application of the "admission load formula" which is promulgated under section 113 and applied to that hospital.

(b) (1) Between April 1 and July 1 of each calendar year beginning with 198__, the Secretary shall promulgate a figure which (subject   to paragraph (2)) shall be the "inpatient hospital revenue increase limit" applicable to the twelve-month period beginning July 1 in such year (with each such twelve-month period being referred to in this title as a "period subject to this title"). Such figure shall be the sum of —

(A) the Hospital Input Price Index (hereinafter in this title referred to as the "HIPI") for the 12-month period ending June 30 of such year, and

(B) one-third of the difference between—

(i) the average annual rate of increase in total hospital expenditures which is found by the Secretary to have occurred during the twenty-four-month period ending on the day preceding January 1 of such calendar year, and

(ii) the annual rate of increase in the HIPI for the twenty-four month period ending on the day preceding January 1 of such calendar year.

(2) If the Secretary finds during any period subject to this title that the HIPI with respect to such period is expected to exceed by more than 1 percentage point the HIPI which was used in making the determination under paragraph (1) (or making a prior adjustment under this paragraph), the Secretary shall increase (or further increase) the HIPI so used by the amount of such excess; except that no adjustment made under this paragraph shall be effective with respect to any accounting year ending prior to the calendar quarter preceding the calendar quarter in which such adjustment is made.

PROMULGATION OF ADMISSION LOAD FORMULA

Section. 113. The admission load formula shall be promulgated by the Secretary by July 1, 198__, and shall be such that—

(1) a hospital will be allowed an increase in total revenue from inpatient services in any accounting year to the extent (and only to the extent) consistent with the inpatient hospital revenue increase limit promulgated under section 112(b), for the period in which such accounting year or any part thereof falls if admissions in such accounting year have increased by less than 2 per centum or declined by less than 6 per centum as compared to the base accounting year (2 per centum and 10 per centum, respectively, in the case of a hospital with no more than four thousand admissions in the base accounting year);

(2) in the case of a hospital whose admissions in any accounting year are beyond the applicable range set forth in paragraph (1), the amount of total revenue from inpatient services in such year which is otherwise allowed under paragraph (1) shall be further increased for each admission above such range by one-half of the average revenue per admission that would have been allowed under paragraph (1) if the actual percentage change in admissions (as compared to the base accounting year) had been zero, or shall be reduced for each admission below such range by one-half of the average revenue per admission that would have been so allowed, except as provided in paragraph (3); and

(3) in the case of a hospital which had more than four thousand admissions in the base accounting year, no additional revenue will be allowed for increased admissions (with respect to any accounting year) beyond 15 per centum above those in the base accounting year, but the revenue otherwise permitted such a hospital under paragraphs (1) and (2) shall be reduced (dollar for dollar) for decreased admissions (in that year) beyond 15 per centum below those in the base accounting year.

BASE INPATIENT HOSPITAL REVENUE

Section. 114. (a) (1) The revenue base for application of the adjusted inpatient hospital revenue increase limit with respect to any hospital in any accounting year shall (subject to subsection (b)) be the revenue from reimbursement due and inpatient charges imposed for inpatient hospital services provided in the hospital's base acounting year (as defined in the hospital's base accounting year (as defined in paragraph (2)).

(2) For purposes of this title, a hospital's "base accounting year" is its accounting year which ended in 198__ or, in the case of a hospital which did not meet the definition contained in section 121 for at least one full accounting year prior to an accounting year ending in 198__ in which it met such definition, the accounting period immediately prior to the first accounting year in which it satisfied such definition.

(b) The base revenue established for any hospital by subsection (a) shall (except as provided in subsection (c)) be reduced by an amount equal to any inpatient charges in such base accounting year for elements of inpatient services for which payment is not made to the hospital in an accounting year any part of which falls within a period subject to this title.

(c) The base revenue established for any hospital by subsection (a) shall be increased to the extent necessary, as determined by the Secretary, to disallow that portion due to unusually low utilization rates in the base year.

(d) Subsection (b) shall not apply with respect to revenue for inpatient services which have been found inappropriate under section 1523(a)(6) of the Public Health Service Act by the State health planning and development agency designated under section 1521 of such Act for the State in which the hospital involved is located.

ESTABLISHMENT OF EXCEPTIONS

Sec. 115. (a) The Secretary shall have authority to grant exceptions from the limits established under this title to individual hospitals for particular periods, but in any case only to the extent that the hospital requesting the exception provides evidence satisfactory to the Secretary—

(1) of the extent to which costs of providing inpatient hospital services in an accounting year any part of which falls within a period subject to this title exceed such costs in the base accounting year as the result of—

(A) changes in admissions beyond the range specified in section 113(3), or

(B) changes in capacity or in the character of inpatient services available in the hospital or major renovation or replacement of physical plant, but only if such changes have increased inpatient costs per admission by more than one-third of the difference specified in section 112(b)(1)(B) over inpatient care costs per admission in the previous accounting year;

(2) that the revenue otherwise allowable (taking into account all other available resources) is insufficient to assure the solvency of the hospital as indicated by the existence of a current ratio of assets to liabilities (determined in accordance with the last sentence of this subsection) of less than the ratio which the Secretary estimates is being experienced by 25 per centum or less of the hospitals subject to this title; and

(3) that the changes in admissions, capacity, plant, or services available generating the excess costs described in paragraph (1) have been found to be needed under section 1523 (a)(5) of the Public Health Service Act or appropriate under section 1523 (a)(6) of the Public Health Service Act by the State health planning and development agency, designated under section 1521 of such Act for the State in which the hospital involved is located.

For purposes of paragraph (2), the term "current ratio of assets to liabilities", with respect to any hospital, means the sum of cash, notes and accounts receivable (less reserves for bad debts), marketable securities, and inventories held by such hospital divided by the sum of all liabilities of such hospital falling due in an accounting year for which the exception is requested under this section.

(b) The Secretary shall either approve any request for an exception made by a hospital under subsection (a), or deny such request, within a period not to exceed ninety days after the hospital has filed in a manner and form prescribed by the Secretary the evidence required by such subsection. Any such request not denied within such ninety-day period shall be deemed approved.

(c) Any hospital granted an exception under this section must make itself available for an operational review by the Secretary. The findings from any such review shall be made public, and continuance of the exception shall be contingent on implementation of any recommendations which may be made (as a result of such operational review) for improvements to increase efficiency and economy.

(d)(1) If the Secretary grants an exception with respect to any accounting year to a hospital which had 4,000 or more admissions in the base accounting year on the grounds set forth in subsection (a)(1)(A), such hospital shall be allowed increased revenue for purposes of this title as though it were a hospital with fewer than four thousand admissions in such base year under section 113.

(2) If the Secretary grants an exception with respect to any accounting year to a hospital on the grounds set forth in subsection (a)(1)(B), such hospital shall be allowed increased total revenue for purposes of this title for such accounting year and all subsequent accounting years (and the limit on its allowable rate of increase in inpatient hospital revenues shall be adjusted upward accordingly) in an amount no greater than the amount necessary to maintain the current ratio of its assets to liabilities (determined in accordance with the last sentence of subsection (a)) at the level specified in subsection (a)(2).

(e)(1) Any hospital which is dissatisfied with a determination of the Secretary under this section may obtain a hearing before the Provider Reimbursement Review Board established under section 1878 of the Social Security Act, if the amount in controversy is $25,000 or more and the request for such hearing is filed within one hundred and eighty days after receipt of the Secretary's determination.

(2) For purposes of paragraph (1), the Secretary (notwithstanding section 1878(h) of the Social Security Act) shall appoint five additional members to the Provider Reimbursement Review Board, following the specifications for expertise applicable to the existing five members. Such five additional members shall constitute the Board for purposes of reviewing appeals under this title. All the other provisions of section 1878 of the Social Security Act shall apply except that the Board as so constituted shall be considered as reviewing decisions of the Secretary rather than of a fiscal intermediary, and subsection (b) of such section shall not apply.

ENFORCEMENT

Sec. 116. (a) Notwithstanding any provision of Title XVIII of the Social Security Act, reimbursement for inpatient hospital services under the program established by that title shall not be payable, on an interim basis or in final settlement, to the extent that it exceeds the applicable limits established under this title.

(b) Notwithstanding any provision of Title V or XIX of such Act, payment shall not be required to be made by any State under either such title with respect to any amount paid for inpatient hospital services in excess of the applicable limits established under this title; nor shall payment be made to any State under either such title with respect to any amount paid for inpatient hospital services in excess of such limits.

(c) Notwithstanding any other provision of law, receipt by any hospital of payment for inpatient hospital services in excess of the applicable limits established under this title, or payment by any cost payer (as defined in section 122(e)(2)) for inpatient hospital services on a cost basis in excess of such limits, shall subject such hospital or cost payer—

(1) to the Federal excise tax imposed by section 4991 of the Internal Revenue Code of 1954 (as added by section 128 of this Act), and

(2) to exclusion, at the discretion of the Secretary, from participation in any or all of the programs established by Titles V, XVIII, and XIX of the Social Security Act.

(d)(1) Where the Secretary determines that average charges per admission billed for inpatient services by a hospital during an accounting year any part of which is included in a period subject to this title exceed the applicable limits established under this title, he shall promulgate (or shall require the hospital to promulgate in such manner as he may prescribe) the percentage by which the average charge per admission billed in that accounting year by the hospital exceeded the applicable limitation on average charges per admission established under this title.

(2) Any hospital described in paragraph (1) shall be exempt from the penalties set forth in subsection (c) if it holds in escrow an amount equal to the percentage promulgated under such paragraph multiplied by the hospital's total inpatient charges less its inpatient charges applicable to cost payers (as defined in section 122(e)), imposed on the accounting year referred to in such paragraph, until such time as charges below the applicable limits established under this title, equal in the aggregate to such amount, are experienced; but any such hospital which fails to do so shall be subject to such penalties.

EXEMPTION FOR HOSPITALS IN CERTAIN STATES

Sec. 117. (a) At the request of the Governor (or other chief executive) of any State (including the District of Columbia and Puerto Rico) the Secretary may exclude from the application of this title all hospitals physically located in such State if the Secretary finds that—

(1) such State has had in effect for at least one year as of the date of such request a program for containing hospital costs in the State which covers at least 90 per centum of the hospitals in the State which would otherwise be covered under the program established by this title;

(2) the State program applies at least to all inpatient care revenues of such hospitals (except revenues received under Title XVIII of the Social Security Act);

(3) the Governor (or chief executive) certifies, and the Secretary determines, that the aggregate rate of increase in inpatient hospital revenues for all hospitals in the State will not exceed the rate promulgated by the Secretary under section 112(b); and

(4) the Governor (or chief executive) has submitted, and had approved by the Secretary, a plan for recovering any excess of revenue which (notwithstanding paragraph (3)) may occur.

(b) A State which would meet the conditions of this section except that its program does not satisfy subsection of (a)(2), but whose program did cover at least 50 per centum of all inpatient care revenues during the twelve-month period preceding the date of its request under subsection (a), will nonetheless be eligible under this section if, by the date of such request, it does have a program which satisfies such subsection.

EXEMPTION FOR HOSPITALS ENGAGED IN CERTAIN EXPERIMENTS OR DEMONSTRATIONS

Sec. 118. A hospital may be excluded from the application of this title if the Secretary determines that (1) such exclusion is necessary to facilitate an experiment or demonstration entered into under section 402 of the Social Security Amendments of 1967 or section 222 of the Social Security Amendments of 1972, and (2) such experiment or demonstration is consistent with the purposes of this title.

PART C—DEFINITIONS AND MISCELLANEOUS PROVISIONS DEFINITION OF HOSPITAL

Sec. 121. (a) For purposes of this title (subject to subsection (b) of this section), the term "hospital", with respect to any accounting year, means an institution (including a distinct part of an institution participating in the program established under Title XVIII of the Social Security Act) which—

(1) satisfies paragraphs (1) and (7) of section 1861(e) of the Social Security Act, and

(2) had an average duration of stay of thirty days or less in the preceding accounting year.

(b) An institution shall not be considered a "hospital" during any part of a period subject to this title if with respect to such period it—

(1) is a Federal hospital;

(2) has met the conditions specified in subsection (a) (under present and previous ownership) for less-than two years before such period; or

(3) derived more than 75 per centum of its inpatient care revenues on a capitation basis, disregarding revenues received under Title XVIII of the Social Security Act, from one or more health maintenance organizations (as defined in section 1301(a) of the Public Health Service Act).

OTHER DEFINITIONS

Sec. 122. For purposes of this title—

Accounting Year

(a) The term "accounting year" with respect to any period means—

(1) in the case of a hospital participating in the program established by Title XVIII of the Social Security Act, a period of twelve consecutive full calendar months including the same months as the last full reporting period allowed for reimbursement purposes under such title;

(2) in the case of a hospital not participating in the program established by Title XVIII of the Social Security Act, a period of twelve consecutive full calendar months including the same months as the last full accounting period used by such other cost payer as the Secretary may designate; and

(3) in the case of a hospital which is not participating in the program established by Title XVIII of the Social Security Act and for which the Secretary does not designate an accounting year under paragraph (2), a calendar year.

Inpatient Hospital Services
(b) The term "inpatient hospital services" has the meaning given it by section 1861(b) of the Social Security Act (including in addition the services otherwise excluded by paragraph (5) thereof).

Inpatient Charges
(c) The term "inpatient charges" means regular rates, applied to all inpatient hospital services, that meet the requirements of section 405.452(d)(4) of the Federal regulations applicable to Title XVIII of the Social Security Act.

Admissions
(d) The term "admission" means the formal acceptance of an inpatient by a hospital, excluding newborn children (unless retained after discharge of the mother) and transfers within inpatient units of the same institution.

Cost Payer
(e) The term "cost payer" means—
(1) a program established by or under Title V, XVIII, or XIX of the Social Security Act, and
(2) any organization which (A) meets the definition contained in section 1842(f)(1) of the Social Security Act, and (B) reimburses a hospital subject to this title for inpatient hospital services on the basis of cost as defined for purposes of such reimbursement.

DETERMINATION OF INPATIENT REIMBURSEMENT

Sec. 123. For purposes of section 111, inpatient reimbursement under the programs established by Titles V, XVIII, and XIX of the Social Security Act shall be determined without regard to adjustments resulting from the application of section 405.460(g),405.455(d), 405.415(f), or 405.415(d)(3) of the Federal regulations applicable to such Title XVIII.

EXEMPTION OF NONSUPERVISORY PERSONNEL WAGE INCREASES FROM REVENUE LIMIT

Sec. 124. (a) At the request of any hospital which is subject to the provisions of this title and which provides the data necessary for the required calculation, the Secretary shall modify the inpatient hospital revenue increase limit and the adjusted inpatient hospital revenue increase limit otherwise established for such hospital with respect to any accounting year under section 112 to allow such hospital to receive, without restriction, revenue equal to the average amount of any increase in regular wages granted in such year to employees who do not meet the definition of "supervisor" as that term is used for purposes of the National Labor Relations Act and (if not employees of a State or political subdivision thereof) who are covered by such Act.
(b) Such modified limits for any accounting year shall be calculated by adding together—
(1) the average percentage increase in regular wages granted to the employees referred to in subsection (a) since the close of the preceding

accounting year multiplied by the percentage of total inpatient cost (as determined for purposes of title XVIII of the Social Security Act) attributable to such wages in such preceding year; and

(2) the inpatient hospital revenue increase limit or, as appropriate, the adjusted inpatient hospital revenue increase limit otherwise applicable to the hospital under this title multiplied by the percentage of revenues (as determined for purposes of Title XVIII of the Social Security Act) attributable to all other expenses in the preceding accounting year.

(c) The modified inpatient hospital revenue increase limit and adjusted inpatient hospital revenue increase limit established under subsection (b) for any hospital with respect to any accounting year shall constitute such hospital's inpatient hospital revenue increase limit or, as appropriate, the adjusted inpatient hospital revenue increase limit for such year under section 111 for all of the purposes of this title.

(d) This section shall apply to accounting years beginning after June 30, 198__, only to the extent the Secretary so determines.

DISCLOSURE OF FISCAL INFORMATION

Sec. 125. (a)(1) Every hospital shall (A) submit semiannually to the health systems agency designated under section 1515 of the Public Health Service Act for the health service area in which it is located, by January 1 and July 1 of each year, its average semiprivate room rate and the charges for the 10 other services which the health system agency finds represent the services which are most frequently used or most important for purposes of comparing hospitals, and make available all cost reports submitted to cost payers, and (B) submit annually its overall plan and budget described in section 1864(z) of the Social Security Act.

(2) Failure by any hospital to comply with the requirement of paragraph (1) shall subject it to exclusion, at the discretion of the Secretary, from participation in any or all of the programs established by Titles V, XVIII, and XIX of the Social Security Act.

(b) Each health systems agency designated under section 1515 of the Public Health Service Act shall publish every January 1 and July 1, in readily understandable language for public use, the information it receives under this section, in a manner designed to facilitate comparisons among hospitals in its area.

IMPROPER CHANGES IN ADMISSION PRACTICES

Sec. 126. Upon written complaint by any institution meeting the conditions set forth in paragraphs (1) and (7) of section 1861(e) of the Social Security Act that one or more hospitals subject to this title in a health service area for which a health systems agency has been designated under section 1515 of the Public Health Service Act has changed its admission practices in an manner that would tend to reduce the proportion of inpatients of such hospital or hospitals for whom reimbursement at less than the inpatient charges (as defined in section 122(c) of this Act) applicable to such inpatients is anticipated, such health systems agency shall investigate the complaint and, upon a finding by such agency that the complaint is justified, the Secretary may impose the sanction set forth in section 116(c)(2) of this Act.

REVIEW OF CERTAIN DETERMINATIONS

Sec. 127. Any determinations made on behalf of the Secretary under this title with respect to the application of its provisions to individual hospitals (other than determinations made under section 115 or 126) shall be subject to the provisions of section 1878 of the Social Security Act in the same manner as determinations with respect to the amount of reimbursement due a provider of services under Title XVIII of such Act.

EXCISE TAX ON EXCESSIVE PAYMENTS FOR INPATIENT HOSPITAL SERVICES

Sec. 128. (a) Subtitle D of the Internal Revenue Code of 1954 (relating to miscellaneous excise taxes) is amended by adding at the end thereof the following new chapter:

"CHAPTER 45—TAX ON CERTAIN EXCESSIVE PAYMENTS FOR INPATIENT HOSPITAL SERVICES

"Sec. 4991. Imposition of tax.

"SEC. 4991. IMPOSITION OF TAX.

"(a) IN GENERAL.—There is hereby imposed, with respect to the receipt by any hospital of payment for inpatient hospital services in excess of the applicable limits established by Title I of the Hospital Cost Containment Act of 198__, and with respect to any payment made by any cost payer as defined in section 122(e)(2) of such Act for inpatient hospital services on a cost basis in excess of such limits, a tax equal to 150 percent of the amount of such excess. The tax imposed by this subsection shall be paid by the hospital or cost payer.

" EXCEPTION.—The tax imposed by subsection (a) shall not apply with respect to any hospital so long as it is determined by the Secretary to be taking the corrective action described in section 16(d)(2) of the Hospital Cost Containment Act of 198__.

"(c) DEFINITIONS.—Terms used in subsections (a) and (b) have the meanings given them by Title I of the Hospital Cost Containment Act of 198__.

"(d) ADMINISTRATION.—Under and to the extent provided by regulations of the Secretary, the appropriate provisions of subtitle F (relating to procedure and administration) shall be made applicable with respect to the tax imposed by subsection (a) of this section.".

(b) The table of chapters for subtitle D of such Code is amended by adding at the end thereof the following new item:

"Chapter 45. Tax on certain excessive payments for
inpatient hospital services."

TITLE II—DETERMINING REASONABLE HOSPITAL COSTS

Sec. 201. Criteria for Determining Reasonable Cost of Hospital Services [Sec. 1861(aa)]

"(aa)(1) To more fairly and effectively determine reasonable costs incurred in providing hospital services, the Secretary shall, not later than April 1, 198__, after consulting with appropriate national organizations, establish—

"(A) an accounting and uniform functional cost reporting system (including uniform procedures for allocation of costs) for determining operating and capital costs of hospitals providing services, and

"(B) a system of hospital classification under which hospitals furnishing services will initially be classified as follows:

"(i)   by size, with each of the following groups of hospitals being classified in separate categories:

(I) those having more than 5, but fewer than 25, beds, (II) those having more than 24, but fewer than 50, beds, (III) those having more than 49, but fewer than 100, beds, (IV) those having more than 99, but fewer than 200, beds, (V) those having more than 199, but fewer than 300, beds, (VI) those having more than 299, but fewer than 400, beds, (VII) those having more than 399, but fewer than 500, beds, and (VIII) those having more than 499 beds,

"(ii)   by type of hospital, with (I) short-term general hospitals being in a separate category, (II) hospitals which are the primary affiliates of accredited medical schools (with one hospital to be nominated by each accredited medical school) being in one separate category (without regard to bed size), and (III) psychiatric, geriatric, maternity, pediatric, or other specialty hospitals being in the same or separate categories, as the Secretary may determine appropriate, in light of any differences in specialty which significantly affect the routine costs of the different types of hospitals, and

"(iii)   other criteria which the Secretary may find appropriate, including modification of bed-size categories;

but the system of hospital classification shall not differentiate between hospitals on the basis of ownership.

"(2) The term 'routine operating costs' used in this subsection does not include:

"(A) capital and related costs,

"(B) costs of interns, residents, and non-administrative physicians,

"(D) energy costs associated with heating and cooling the hospital plant, and

"(E) malpractice insurance expense, or,

"(F) ancillary service costs.

"(3)(A) During the calendar quarter beginning on January 1 of each year, beginning with 198__, the Secretary shall determine, for the hospitals in each category of the system established under paragraph (1)(B), an average per diem routine operating cost amount weighted by the ratio of admissions per diem to admissions per diem during the base year, but in no case greater than one, which shall (except as otherwise provided in this subsection) be used in determining payments to hospitals.

"(B) The determination shall be based upon the amount of the hospitals' routine operating costs for the preceding fiscal year.

"(C) In making a determination, the routine operating costs of each hospital shall be divided into personnel and nonpersonnel components.

"(D) (i) The personnel and nonpersonnel components of routine operating costs for each of the hospitals (other than for those excluded under clause (ii)) in eash category shall be added for all hospitals and then divided by the total number of days of routine care provided by the hospitals in the category to determine the average per diem routine operating cost of each category.

(ii) In making the calculations required by clause (i), the Secretary shall exclude any hospital which has significant understaffing or which otherwise experiences significant cost differentials resulting from failure of the hospital to fully meet the standards and conditions of participation as a provider of services as determined by the Secretary.

"(E) There shall be determined for each hospital in each category a a weighted per diem payment rate for routine operating costs. That payment rate shall equal the average per diem routine operating cost amount for the category in which the hospital is expected to be classified during the subsequent fiscal year weighted by the ratio of admissions per diem during the base year to admissions per diem in the current year, but in no case greater than one, except that the personnel component shall be adjusted using a wage index based upon general wage levels (including fringe benefit costs) in the areas in which the hospitals are located. If the Secretary finds that, in an area where one or more hospitals in any category are located, for the fiscal year ending June 30, 198__, the wage level (including fringe benefit costs) for hospitals is significantly higher than the general wage level (including fringe benefit costs) in that area (relative to the relationship between hospital wages and general wages in other areas), then the general wage level in the area shall be deemed equal to the wage level for hospitals in that area, but only during fiscal year 198__.

"(4)(A) (i) The term 'adjusted weighted per diem payment rate for routine operating costs', means the weighted per diem payment rate for routine operating costs plus the average percentage increase in prices determined under Section 112.

"(ii) In making payments for services, the Secretary shall add a semiannual average percentage increase in the cost of the mix of goods and services (including personnel and nonpersonnel costs) comprising routine operating costs, equal to the lesser of: (I) the average percentage increase estimated by the hospital, or (II) the average percentage increase in the area estimated by the Secretary.

"(iii) At the end of the fiscal year, the amounts paid under clause (ii) shall be adjusted to reflect the lesser of (I) the actual cost increase experienced by the hospital or (II) the actual increase in costs which occurred in the mix of goods and services in the area. Adjustments shall also be made to take account of unexpected changes in the hospital's classification.

"(B) For purposes of payment the amount of routine operating cost incurred by a hospital shall be deemed to equal—

"(i) for a hospital which has actual routine operating costs equal to or greater than that hospital's adjusted weighted per diem payment rate for routine operating costs, an amount equal to the greater of:

"(I) The hospital's actual routine operating costs, but not exceeding 120 percent of the hospital's adjusted weighted per diem payment rate for routine operating costs, or

"(II) the amounts determined for the hospital under clause (I) if it had been classified in the bed-size category nearest to the category in which the hospital was classified, but not exceeding the hospital's actual routine operating costs; and

"(ii) for a hospital which has actual routine operating costs less than that hospital's adjusted weighted per diem payment rate for routine operating costs, an amount equal to (I) the amount of the hospital's actual routine operating costs, plus (II) whichever is smaller: (a) 5 percent of the hospital's adjusted weighted per diem payment rate for routine operating costs, or (b) 50 percent of the amount by which the hospital's adjusted per year diem payment rate for routine operating costs exceeds the hospital's actual routine operating costs.

"(C) Any hospital excluded by the Secretary under paragraph (3)(D)(ii), shall be reimbursed for routine operating costs the lesser of (i) actual costs or (ii) the reimbursement determined under this subsection.

"(D) April 1 of the year in which the Secretary determines the amount of the average weighted per diem operating cost for each hospital category and the adjusted weighted per diem payment rate for each hospital, the determinations shall be published by the Secretary; and the Secretary shall notify the hospital administrator and the administrative governing body of each hospital with respect to all aspects of the determination which affect the hospital.

"(E) If a hospital is determined by the Secretary to be—

"(i) located in an underserved area where hospital services are not otherwise available,

"(ii) certified as being currently necessary by an appropriate planning agency, and

"(iii) underutilized,

the adjusted weighted per diem payment rate shall not apply to that portion of the hospital's routine operating costs attributable to the underutilized capacity.

"(F) If a hospital satisfactorily demonstrates to the Secretary that, in the aggregate, its patients require a substantially greater intensity of care than is generally provided by the other hospitals in the same category, resulting in unusually greater routine operating costs, the the adjusted weighted per diem payment rate shall not apply to that portion of the hospital's routine operating costs attributable to the greater intensity of care required.

(G) The Secretary may further increase the adjusted weighted per diem payment rate to reflect the higher prices prevailing in Alaska or Hawaii.

(H) Where the Secretary finds that a hospital has manipulated its patient mix, or patient flow, or provides less than the normal range and extent of patient service, or where an unusually large proportion of routine nursing service is provided by private-duty nurses, the routine operating costs of that hospital shall be deemed equal to whichever is less: the amount determined without regard to this subsection, or the amount determined under subparagraph (B).

"(5) Where any provisions of this subsection are inconsistent with section 1861(v), this subsection supersedes section 1861(v).

(c)(1) The Secretary shall, at the earliest practical date, develop additional methods for reimbursing hospital's for all other costs, and for reimbursing all other entities which are reimbursed on the basis of reasonable cost. Those methods shall provide appropriate classification and reimbursement systems designed to ordinarily permit comparisons of the cost centers of one entity, either individually or in the aggregate, with cost centers similar in terms of size and scale of operation, prevailing wage levels, nature, extent, and appropriate volume of the services furnished, and other factors which have a substantial impact on hospital costs. The Secretary shall provide procedures for appropriate exceptions.

(2) The systems of reimbursement shall not permit payment for costs which exceed 120 percent of the average cost incurred by other institutions or agencies in the same class, unless an exception has been allowed.

(3) The Secretary shall, as classification and reimbursement systems methods are developed, but not later than two years from enactment, submit appropriate legislative recommendations to the Congress.

(d) The provisions of section 1861(aa) (2), (3), and (4) of the Social Security Act—

(1) shall apply for informational purposes for services furnished by a hospital before July 1, 1981, and

(2) shall be effective for fiscal years beginning with fiscal year 1983.

(e) Notwithstanding any other provision of this Act, where the Secretary has entered into a contract with a State, as authorized under section 222 of Public Law 92–603 or section 1533(d) of the Public Health Service Act, to establish a reimbursement system for hospitals, hospital reimbursement in that State under

Titles XVIII and XIX shall be based on that State system, if the Secretary finds that—

(1) the State has mandated the reimbursement system and it applies to all hospitals in the State which have provider agreements under Title XVIII or Title XIX;

(2) the system applies to all revenue sources for hospital services in the State;

(3) all hospitals in the State with which there is a provider agreement conform to the accounting and uniform reporting requirements of section 1861(aa)(1)(A), and furnishes any appropriate reports that the Secretary may require; and,

(4) (A) based upon an annual evaluation of the system, aggregate payments to hospitals in the State under Title XVIII and Title XIX for those components of hospitals costs determined under section 1861(aa) for the fiscal year following an annual evaluation are estimated to be less than payments would be under section 1861(aa) or, (B) where a State that is unable to satisfy requirements of subparagraph (A) demonstrates to the satisfaction of the Secretary that total reimbursable inpatient hospital costs in the State are lower than would otherwise be payable under Title XVIII and Title XIX.

If the Secretary finds that any of the above conditions in a State which previously met them have not been met for a year the Secretary shall, after due notice, reimburse hospitals in that State according to the provisions of this Act unless he finds that unusual, justifiable and non-recurring circumstances led to the failure to comply.

(f)(1) Section 1866(a)(1) of the Social Security Act is amended by inserting ",and" in place of the period at the end of subparagraph (C), and by adding a subparagraph: "(D) not to increase amounts due from any individual, organization, or agency in order to offset reductions made under section 1861(aa) in the amount paid, or expected to be paid, under Title XVIII.".

(2) Section 1902(a)(27) of the Social Security Act is amended by deleting "and" at the end of subparagraph (A), by inserting ",and" in place of the semicolon at the end of subparagraph (B) and by adding a new subparagraph;

"(C) not to increase amounts due from any individual, organization, or agency in order to offset reductions made under section 1902(a)(13)(D) in the amount paid, or expected to be paid under Title XIX;"

(h) Section 1902(a)(13)(D) is amended to read as follows:

"(D) for payment of the reasonable cost of inpatient hospital services provided under the plan, applying the methods specified in section 1861(v) and section 1861(aa), which are consistent with section 1122; and".

7 Conclusion

Controlling the new inflation will take more than programmatic courage, although it will require much more courage than has been evidenced by recent leaderships. It will also take another equally important but lacking element—a new paradigm which more correctly fits the new inflation than does the paradigm of planned recession followed by renewed, but higher inflation. The courage required is commensurate with the complexity of some of the measures proposed here. If not these measures, then others are required, probably equally ambitious, and certainly directed at the same root causes. For the paradigm presented here, if not the particular programmatic solutions, provides, I think, the closest fit with the causes and effects of the new inflation of any I have seen.[1]

Furthermore, the programmatic elements have considerable practical appeal. Although wage and price controls cannot be the sum total of a direct anti-inflation program, nor can they be a long-run part of one, they are preferable to recession as a short-run part of a basic necessities inflation strategy. Consequently, the model stand-by wage-price control authority set forth here is a legitimate alternative for the immediate period following dramatic OPEC oil price increases, such as occurred in 1973–1974 and 1979–1980.

The national grain price stabilization board proposed here is a long overdue alternative to the recurrent and long enduring effects of international demand fluctuations on the whole pattern of domestic U.S. food production and prices. No doubt, the reader can think of other food-sector reforms: deregulation of food transportation, more aggressive antitrust action against increasing concentration in food processing and marketing, and aid to family farms, for instance. But which of these other programs is as likely as grain export management to have an enduring effect on the general level of food prices (and resultant wage claims)?

Similarly, one can think of many alternative programs to check medical-care inflation, such as regulation of physicians' fees, expanded use of prepaid medical care, consumer jawboning of third-party payers such as Blue Cross. But which of these are any more practical than hospital cost containment? Certainly not regulation of physicians' fees.[2] And my own study of prepaid medical care plans for a major private insurance company led me to conclude that they indirectly offer some hope of reducing the rate of medical cost inflation, but this reduction could be better achieved directly. Leaving aside the debate about the relative quality of prepaid versus fee-for-service care, prepaid plans succeed in reducing cost by restricting access to in-patient hospital care. Except for restricted access to in-patient treatment of sickness that can be treated on an out-patient basis, the mix of inputs used by prepaid plans (professional, administrative, medical technology) is roughly the same as that for fee-for-service plans. With the same mix of inputs (except for out-patient treatment of minor illnesses), both plans experience the same *rate* of inflation. It's a little like substituting a Buick for a Cadillac.

Prepaid plans do tend to draw their new members from a younger and healthier population, but to the extent that is reflected in lower plan costs, it is not a desideratum for societal response to the new inflation. In sum, direct control of hospital cost itself (together with restricted in-patient access where consumers choose it) seems a more efficient anti-inflation alternative.

In the housing sector, any reform is tough. Although there is desperate need for expanded public housing, even that would not significantly ease the devastating effect of the new inflation on the private housing sector and on nonhomeowner, middle-income families. Moreover, housing is a very fractured industry in which the secondary inflationary effects of recession are enormous, due to bankruptcy of builders permanently eliminating some suppliers, and pent-up demand unbottled after easing of tight money. Equity-shared mortgages, proposed here, involve a minimal federal role (incentives to encourage local banks to make equity-shared mortgages available for low- and middle-priced houses). Again, the effect per dollar of government effort appears larger than other possible programs and the governmental involvement less intrusive.

Among the energy alternatives, of course, an aggressive stand-by gasoline rationing scheme seems most controversial. But again it is designed as a short-run alternative to the recessions that followed the 1973–1974 and 1979–1980 jolts. And it should not involve cumbersome coupons for long, since the goal is to quickly substitute tax-rationing for negotiable coupon-rationing. The alternative is unmitigated jolts to $60, $80, $100 per barrel of oil in the 1980s and 1990s. It would be better to conserve by ration coupon or ration tax than to pay OPEC. The money spent to administer rationing would directly aim to reduce demand, creating slack in the oil market and, thus, downward pressure on spot prices.

What would be the overall effect on inflation of the strategies suggested here? It depends, of course, upon a thousand factors, including when the jolts occur, what the growth rate of the economy then is, and when the strategies are implemented, to name a few. Grain price stabilization could virtually eliminate the adverse effects of today's international grain price volatility, thereby steadying the hog and cattle cycles. Reduction in the rate of food-price inflation could be as much as 40 percent depending on the secondary effects on land prices and wage demands.

Equity-shared mortgages, if widely accepted and equal to roughly a one-third for one-third split, could lower house price inflation in the medium-term by an indeterminate amount; my best estimate is by more than a 10 percent reduction in the house price inflation rate—if the practice were widespread and particularly encouraged when interest rates rise sharply.

Hospital cost containment could slow medical care inflation by 20 percent, assuming physicians' salaries continue to inflate at no more than prior high rates.

The evidence suggests that gasoline rationing could possibly halve the short-term direct and secondary inflationary impact of an oil jolt—for say, the fifteen months following the jolt, after which tax rationing could be eased, assuming the other strategies mentioned were in place.

There are signs that in some respects the American economy is adjusting well to the new inflation. Beseiged as we are by Toyotas, Sonys, and Mercedes, we forget that the United States outstripped its two major trading partners from 1970 to 1980, as U.S. companies exported aggressively to help compensate for the cost of oil imports. In 1980, for example, according to the Morgan Guaranty Trust Company, the United States current account—the broadest balance-of-payments measure, including merchandise trade as well as services, repatriated overseas profits and short-term capital flows— showed a surplus of $4 billion, despite OPEC imports, in contrast to the 1970 surplus of $2.3 billion. At the same time, Germany (in the midst of a severe recession) and Japan (narrowly skirting one) showed current account deficits in 1980 of $16 and $12 billion, respectively, as compared to their respective 1970 surpluses of $.7 billion and $2 billion. We forget about American aircraft and agricultural exports, for example. Indeed, our understandable subsidy since World War II of the defense of those two countries (last year the U.S. spent $520 per person on defense, while Japan spent only $87 and West Germany $266) and our cheap and enormous grain exports, described in this book, underwrite the economies of West Germany and Japan, improving their competitive positions above what they otherwise would be. More aggressive U.S. exporting is, however, a sign of strength amid overwhelming evidence of stagnation. Stagnation will continue so long as inflation remains a barrier to full employment policies and a growing economic pie.

Assuming that the various sectoral strategies and stand-by wage-price authority were available to be used in combination, we might expect the general level of inflation in the United States over the next decade to be one-third below what it otherwise would be. Equally important, we might expect a climate of more stable expectations of steadier growth to develop, in contrast to today's psychology of accelerating cycles of necessity price jolts–inflation–recession–jolts. Thereby, expectations would reinforce the improving trend toward steadier growth (on which increasing productivity and a rising standard of living depend). Controlling the new inflation, as much as these reforms could do, could be enough to turn the tide of expectations in America. And, as Keynes said, life is all a question of expectations.

Notes

1. See appendix A for a rebuttal of critiques by Thurow and Minarik.
2. The AMA had one of the largest of all political action committees providing funds to political candidates in the 1980 election.

Postscript:
From Economic
Stabilization to
Economic Development

"I should like to buy an egg please," she said timidly. *"How do you sell them?" "Fivepence farthing for one—two pence for two,"* the Sheep replied. *"Then two are cheaper than one?"* Alice said in a surprised tone, taking out her purse. *"Only you must eat them both, if you buy two,"* said the Sheep. *"Then I'll have one, please,"* said Alice as she put the money down on the counter. For she thought to herself, *"They mightn't be nice at all, you know."*
      —Lewis Carroll, *Through the Looking Glass.*

Uncertain expectations can lead to underinvestment, especially if interest rates, oil prices, and food prices continue to jump unexpectedly. This book offers some ideas to help stabilize those prices and thereby improve the climate for investment. But the ideas presented here are only part of a liberal economic agenda. Inflation and recurrent recession have so weakened America's heavy-industrial base—those traditionally basic industries stretching from Baltimore to St. Louis—that many will remain weak and uncompetitive in international markets if unassisted. During the 1970s, nearly one million manufacturing jobs were lost in the Baltimore-St. Louis industrial region. American capitalism (although strong in areas of grain export, coal reserves, development of high technology, and growth of services) is suffering from a crisis of capital. Estimated credit demand in 1981 exceeded $410 billion, up 33 percent from 1980, pushing total debt outstanding to more than $4 trillion.[1] As return to stockholders's equity shrank with lower corporate earnings in the 1970s, investors shifted out of the basic-industry stocks (except energy) putting pressure on debt-equity ratios. Whereas the market provided industry with just $70 billion in new equity capital in the 1970s, the need is estimated to be almost four times that in the 1980s, and the outlook is no brighter.

Meanwhile, capital is now being drained from this country at a staggering rate of $500 billion every five years—nearly half the present value of all companies listed on the New York Stock Exchange— in order to pay OPEC. The OPEC countries keep much of this money in short-term notes, unable to use it for domestic investment and unwilling to risk it to the perils of the inflation they helped generate by lending it for longer terms.

A key political-economic question for the 1980s is whether the OPEC countries can be induced to lend to an agency such as the International Bank for Reconstruction and Development (the World Bank) some of the

$300 billion in excess of their own needs they will accumulate over the decade in order to capitalize Reconstruction and Development Banks in member countries. Felix Rohatyn suggested something similar to this when he called for re-creation of a Reconstruction Finance Corporation (RFC), capitalized at $5 billion by Congress and authorized to sell $25 billion in federally guaranteed bonds (possibly, in part, to OPEC). The RFC would buy equity in ailing industries when necessary (but not more than 50 percent of any project) and sell its stock on the market as soon as practicable.[2] Obviously, creation of such an RFC depends in part on finding an external market for $25 billion in bonds. Otherwise, increased federal borrowing would put added pressure on private borrowers. However, if this obstacle can be overcome, an RFC appears far preferable to the current congressional response exemplified by the huge and expensive additional debt provided to Chrysler, already crushed with debt, in return for inadequate management and labor concessions. Is an RFC "state capitalism"? Rohatyn, a successful banker, says no. It seems clear, however, that it is a temporary form of state capitalism, raising serious questions about how democratic controls could be brought to bear on the government's exercise of influence concomitant to its stock ownership in companies aided by an RFC.[3] Perhaps in this decade the themes of economic stabilization, economic development, and economic democracy will merge in a program for the strengtening of capitalism.

Notes

1. George F. Will, "Facing Up to Reality," *Boston Globe,* February 16, 1981 at 15.
2. Felix Rohatyn "Reconstructing America," *New York Review of Books,* March 5, 1981 at 16.
3. For the tools of analysis (but not a discussion of democratic control), *see* I.M.D. Little and J.A. Mirrlees, *Project Appraisal and Planning for Developing Countries,* (New York: Basic Books, 1974.).

Appendix:
Response to
Minarik and Thurow

Joseph J. Minarik of the Brookings Institution has asserted that the vast majority of the population benefits from inflation and that the rich are the biggest losers. This rather startling conclusion flows from incorporating into his analysis the effects of inflation, not only on prices, but on incomes as well. (Minarik defines the latter to include changes in net wealth). Summarizing liberally, Minarik's conclusions are that the poor are not seriously hurt by inflation, the middle class benefits, and the rich are seriously hurt. These conclusions flow from the assumptions:

1. Welfare benefits are more or less adequately indexed to the cost of living.
2. Wages and salaries are also adequately indexed to the cost of living.
3. For the middle class, the appreciation of home values and fixed nominal mortgage payments more than compensates for the effect of inflation on tax rates ("bracket creep").
4. For the rich, higher interest rates that result from inflation do not compensate for the erosion of the principal value of bonds. The lag of depreciation allowances behind machinery replacement costs similarly reduces the real value of the other principal form of wealth of the rich, stocks.

While the analysis has considerable validity, it is unfortunate that its conclusions have been widely circulated without attention to the assumption and methodology. Minarik's conclusions about the effects of inflation on the poor, middle class, and the rich are not based on empirical analysis of what, in fact, happened to prices and incomes during the recent period of inflation, but rather are the result of a simulation of the personal income distribution under certain assumptions about how flows of different forms of income are affected by inflation *in general*. While the methodology is quite sophisticated in that it simulates the entire income and wealth distribution, Minarik's conclusions flow fairly straightforwardly from these assumptions with few surprising results. Consequently, it is the assumptions that must be subjected to scrutiny in order to evaluate both the validity of the model and the "fit" between the model and the actual reality of inflation over the past few years. Many of the assumptions about income flows seem open to questions, but more important are implicit assumptions about what constitutes economic benefit "income" and "hurt".

Perhaps the most important, and at the same time dubious, assumption in the model is that labor income is perfectly and completely indexed to the overall rate of inflation with no lag. This assumption virtually guarantees the conclusion that the middle class, primarily dependent upon labor for income, will not be hurt by inflation. While wages certainly do attempt to catch up with the rate of inflation (that is, a 10 percent increase in the price level would rarely result in a 10 percent reduction in purchasing power), there are undoubtedly lags and substantial periods (for instance, 1978-1979) when real wages fall. The model also implicitly assumes that workers at the low end of the wage distribution are as successful as those in the primary industrial sectors in achieving wage gains that keep them even with inflation. This seems unlikely, and it is also definitely true that the minimum wage level has lagged substantially behind the rate of inflation in recent years, as have the wages of governmental employees, particularly at the state and local level.

Another questionable assumption is that transfer payments are well indexed for inflation. While this is somewhat true of Social Security and Food Stamps (Minarik does account here for lags) his statement that for "the most prominent welfare program, aid to families with dependent children...the best available evidence indicates that benefits in most states kept pace with prices through the recent burse of inflation"[1] is clearly mistaken. The best available evidence concluded that the recent inflation had caused a substantial decline in real AFDC benefits in nearly every state for which data was available.

In addition to these two questionable assumptions about the behavior of income flows, there are problems with Minarik's income concepts. First, for an unexplained reason (perhaps because of a lack of available data) Minarik does not count realized capital gains as income; if an individual makes a profit in the real estate market, Minarik's model does not capture this income source. It would seem highly likely that in an inflationary period in which, according to Minarik's own analysis, stocks and bonds are poor inflation hedges, many more wealthy individuals would be investing in tangible objects (gold, real estate) and realizing capital gains on the investment. Not counting this as income would seem to be a clear source of bias. It is an especially serious shortcoming in the model given the fact that Minarik *does* include as income unrealized capital gains from the appreciation of home values. This "income" source is the major reason that, according to Minarik, the middle class not only is not harmed by inflation but actually benefits.

The latter point leads to the broader issue of implicit assumptions in Minarik's analysis about what constitutes economic benefit, income and hurt (as in: "the rich are hurt the most by inflation"). For example, one of the reasons that Minarik concludes that the poor are not substantially hurt by inflation is that many low-income elderly persons who own their own homes obtain income, in Minarik's definition, when their homes appreciate in value. Yet it is more likely that people in this situation are hurt by the higher property taxes that result; actual income will accrue only to their children when they inherit the house. Likewise, the major reason that Minarik concludes that the rich are hurt by inflation is that capital losses occur on bonds. Yet does the erosion of real wealth, which undeniably occurs, constitute hurt, when it does not force a decline in a standard of living? To his credit, Minarik concludes, "Despite their losses of real income [again, changes in net wealth constituting income in Minarik's definition], upper income households cannot be considered burdened by inflation, simply because their resources are sufficient to cope; policy should be directed not toward any burden, but rather toward economic efficiency."[2] But this again raises broader questions about the relevance of Minarik's entire analysis to policy formulation.

There are many more methodological assumptions and implicit value judgment's in Minarik's analysis that are worthy of scrutiny. Especially important is the broad issue of the relevance of a simulation based on past behavioral relationships to current reality. Are not wealthy people attempting to adjust their investment portfolios to avoid capital losses, for example? Minarik assumes that no options are really available that would enable the rich, as a class, to improve their position vis-a-vis other income groups. Yet is it not possible that, for example, in the past few years those individuals with sufficient resources to invest in money market certificates have been able to maintain the real value of their savings at the expense of lower-income individuals who were trapped into 5 percent passbooks? As a simulation, Minarik's analysis does not and cannot assess changing behavior in response to changing reality.

Because of the rigidity of its underlying assumptions, the ability to make firm statements about what groups are and aren't hurt by actual (as opposed to simulated) inflation, let alone how badly, based solely on this analysis, seems highly problematic. Nevertheless, Minaraik's work is useful in emphasizing that the reality of inflation is complex and the effects should not be oversimplified: rich people are suffering capital losses on some investments, some workers are keeping ahead of inflation and many others are keeping even, homeowners do benefit from the fixed nominal value of mortgage payments, and some may be able to translate the appreciation of their equity that results from inflation into a higher standard of living.

Another related argument advanced by Minarik is that the basic necessities index complied by the National Center for Economic Alternatives inaccurately indicates that inflation in necessity items is more severe and thus the poor, who spend a larger fraction of their incomes on these necessities, are more severely hurt by inflation. But Minarik only obliquely captures one of the two important purposes of the basic necessities index when he states, "The most one can say for it is that it is an index of the prices of the fastest inflating items in the CPI."[3]

Minarik may quibble on the components of the index (a defense of which follows) but in that sentence he inadvertently reflects its primary value as a policy tool. The new inflation is not generalized but rather is being driven by sectoral surges in food, housing, energy, and health. Increasing public recognition of this fact is a primary purpose of the basic necessities index. Minarik himself concluded in *The Review of Income and Wealth,* "If inflation is concentrated in food and fuel products, as was the case in recent years, the losses to low income households are somewhat greater."[4]

Minarik charges that basic necessities inflation is merely a catchy phrase suggesting a quick fix. But the fact is that human thought advances by means of metaphor. In response, I would say that "Necessity is the mother of the new inflation" is admittedly a catchy phrase, but its true importance lies in the fact that it spotlights some of the significance of the surging inflation in food, housing, energy, and health. Old shibboleths about excess demand and other forms of generalized inflation are simply inapposite to today's inflation. Nor does recognition of the sectoral nature of the new inflation lead to any quick fix proscriptions. This book demonstrates that. Minarik's contention that the necessity sectors lag rather than lead other sectors in the timing of price increases is incorrect. The evidence shows that energy and food price jolts push the new inflation, health costs are naggingly steady in their rise, and housing prices alternately lead and lag due to structural volatility.

Turning to Minarik's concern to modify the components of the basic necessities index, his basic criticisms are: the basic necessities index distorts a number of problems in the CPI; it excludes clothing; it overstates the cost of housing to low and middle-income families who are not frequently in the house-buying market; and it doesn't deal with quality changes as in health care.

In response, again, clothing is excluded because inflation in other sectors is more severe, not because clothing is not necessary to living. Incidentally, however, clothing expenditures would appear more postponeable than those included in the basic necessities index.

On the housing component, no answer is completely satisfactory—as all the recent debate about the housing component of the CPI shows. But Minarik's proposal (the rental equivalents index) is much less satisfactory than NCEA's (the cost of buying a home). The rental equivalents index substantially understates the cost of home ownership. It is a survey of rental costs based on apartments, not rental homes. The stock of rental apartments (including many subject to rent control) is different from that of rental homes. Single family homes are sold more frequently than apartments, driving up their prices faster; and more apartments are now sold for tenant ownership (condominium) which excludes them from Minarik's proposed rental equivalent index. In this mobile society, where one family in ten moves each year, and where increasing numbers of baby-boom couples are entering the housing market, the cost of home buying is a significant fact of life for many people. Moreover, the Bureau of Labor Statistics justifies its current housing measure (house buying) on the basis that it measures home-ownership in the same way that ownership of other durable goods is measured in the CPI. Finally, returning to the descriptive purpose of the basic necessities index, it is worth noting that recently the four Bureau of Labor Statistics indices for housing other than the rental equivalents index have all increased faster than the rate of inflation of nonnecessities over the same period. House price inflation is fueling the new inflation.

Minarik accurately points out that the CPI is based on an old survey of consumers and that, wisely, consumers' spending patterns have changed in the past eight years (people eat less steak, more chicken) so the impact of inflation in higher priced foods, for example is overstated in the CPI (and thus in the basic necessities index). But the increases in energy prices since 1972–1973 have resulted in a major change in spending patterns for people in the colder regions of the country. Elderly people have faced large increases in property taxes during the same period despite having low nominal costs of home ownership. In short, Minarik is picking and choosing faults somewhat arbitrarily: all people do not rent, low and middle-income people do eat out at restaurants (especially with the growing fast food craze over the past decade, and as more women work full time), and food and fuel are less postponable than clothing.

Minarik's statements about the improving quality of health care are very clearly misdirected. It is broadly accepted that the CPI *understates* the cost of health care inflation. The weight of health care in the CPI is well under the cost of health care in the economy because the Bureau of Labor Statistics Consumer Expenditure Survey only counts out-of-pocket expenses not employer or government insurance payments which have exploded. So, if anything, the basic necessities index understates health care inflation.

Finally, Minarik's comparison of his improved necessities index with the CPI is flawed by his failure to adjust the CPI yardstick for the decreased cost of housing under his measurement system. If he made those adjustments, even his improved necessities index would remain above the CPI as a whole.

Minarik has importantly focused on the problem of any index. On balance, the basic necessities index appears descriptively accurate (these are the sectors of worst inflation) and prescriptively suggestive.

At this point, we meet Lester Thurow's argument head on. He argues, somewhat similarly to Minarik's analysis referred to at the outset, that inflation has resulted in no real shifts in income. It's all a wash. No one's hurt. No one benefits. But the data Thurow used to argue his case (census-defined income 1972–1977) is incomplete. There have been several years of *severe* inflation since 1977 (including new oil and grain jolts). In arguing that inflation is like a tax on wealth (thus hurting the rich, who have it, more) his census-income definition excludes inflation-bloated capital gains. Nor does he deal with increases in labor-force participation of women to maintain family income levels. And over time, he assumes that low and middle-income people can insulate themselves from inflation as well as the more well-to-do and more powerful. As Paul Blumberg (whom Thurow criticized) has noted, for example, between 1972 and 1974, food prices increased very sharply (CPI for food increased from 124 in 1972 to 162 in 1974, with 1967 equaling 100), possibly the largest two year increase in U.S. history. In this period the lowest income decible increased the proportion of its expenditures on food by over 16 percent, the highest by only 5.6 percent. In general, the bottom half of income earners had to increase their expenditures on food more sharply than did the top half of income earners during this period of rapidly rising food prices. In other words, it's not a wash as Mr. Thurow claims.

The evidence is that the new inflation is concentrated in the sectors liberally defined as the basic necessities: food, housing, energy, and health. Fighting it with generalized budget cuts, tight money, planned recession, or even generalized productivity-enhancing tax incentives will not work. Each of these sectors has unique factors causing its inflation. To each must be directed unique and enlightened policies.

Notes

1. Joseph J. Minarik, "Who Wins, Who Loses From Inflation?", *Brookings Bulletin,* Summer 1978, at 7.

2. Joseph J. Minarik, Prepared Statement before the Task Force on Inflation of the Committee on the Budget, U.S. House of Representatives, *Impact of Inflation on the Economy,* Hearing held June 18, 19, 21 and 22, 1979, pp. 465–472.

3. Joseph J. Minarik, "Inflation in the Necessities?", *Brookings Bulletin,* Spring 1980.

4. Joseph J.Minarik, "The Size Distribution of Income During Inflation," *Review of Income and Wealth,* December 1979, pp. 377–392.

Bach, George L., and Stephenson James B. "Inflation and the Redistribution of Wealth," *Review of Economics and Statistics, 56* February, 1974, 1–13.

Budd, Edward C., and Seiders David F., "The Impact of Inflation on the Distribution of Income and Wealth," *American Economic Review,* May 1971, 128–38.

Minarik Joseph J. "The Size Distribution of Income During Inflation," *The Review of Income and Wealth,* December 1979, 377–392.

———, "Inflation in the Necessities?", *The Brookings Bulletin,* Spring 1980.

———, "Who Wins, Who Loses From Inflation?" *The Brookings Bulletin,* Summer 1978, 6–10.

———,"Proposals to Alleviate Inflation Would Make It Worse," *Washington Post,* March 16, 1980.

———, "Prepared Statement" before the Task Force on Inflation of the Committee on the Budget, U.S. House of Representatives, *Impact of Inflation on the Economy,* Hearing held June 18, 19, 21 and 22, 1979, 465–472.

Thurow, Lester C. "Our Standard of Living Has Not Fallen," *Challenge,* March–April 1980.

———, *The Zero Sum Society; Distribution and the Possibilities for Economic Change,* Basic Books, New York (1980).

Index

About the Author

Thomas J. Dougherty is an associate of the National Center for Economic Alternatives, a public-interest research organization based in Washington, D.C. He is a former Marshall Scholar, Danforth Foundation Fellow, and Woodrow Wilson Fellow. A graduate of The College of the Holy Cross, he received the B.Phil. degree in economics from Oxford University in 1973 and was graduated from Harvard Law School in 1976. He is former managing editor of the *Harvard Journal on Legislation.*